DARK DREAMS

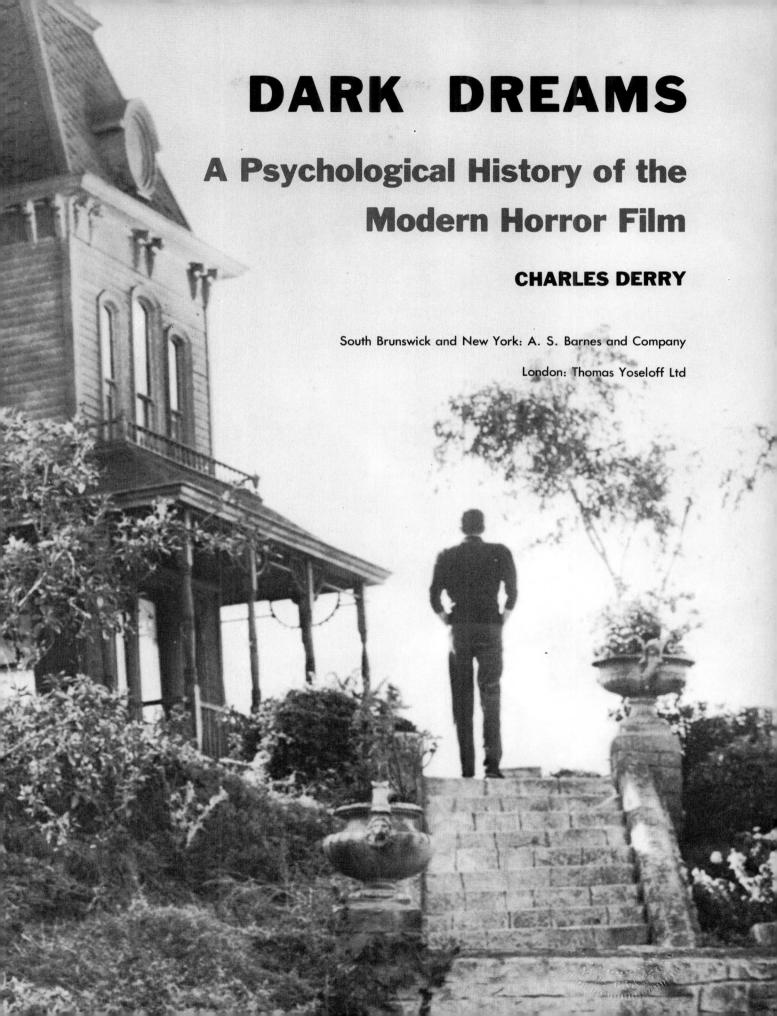

DARK DREAMS

A Psychological History of the Modern Horror Film

CHARLES DERRY

South Brunswick and New York: A. S. Barnes and Company

London: Thomas Yoseloff Ltd

A. S. Barnes and Co., Inc.
Cranbury, New Jersey 08512

Thomas Yoseloff Ltd
Magdalen House
136-148 Tooley Street
London SE1 2TT, England

Library of Congress Cataloging in Publication Data

Derry, Charles, 1951-
Dark dreams.

Bibliography: p.
Includes index.
1. Horror films—History and criticism.
2. Moving-pictures—Psychological aspects.
I. Title.
PN1995.9.H6D38   791.43′0909′16   76-10879
ISBN 0-498-01915-2

PRINTED IN THE UNITED STATES OF AMERICA

to
Charles Homer Derry

CONTENTS

FOREWORD

Now that the auteur theory has faded somewhat from intellectual fashion, taking with it a passion, briefly evident among critics, for dividing filmmakers into the Elect, who could do no wrong, and the rest, mere capable craftsmen who could do precious little right, it has been replaced by a new orthodoxy: genre criticism. The point of this, of course, is that certain stars, certain props, certain situations, have an immediately recognizable significance in certain cinematic contexts. If you cast John Wayne in a Western or Gloria Grahame in a film noir, you are using a sort of shorthand which any seasoned moviegoer can instantly read: their mere presence tells us what sort of a character they are supposed to be and more or less what can be expected of them. But the context of genre is vital: John Wayne in a drawing-room comedy or Gloria Grahame in a musical would be an unknown quantity. In other words, much of genre criticism is concerned with the examination and re-evaluation of cliché: we tend to forget that truisms are, after all, as a rule true.

The problem of genre criticism is generally one of definition. Some genres define themselves by obvious externals: the Western or the musical, for example. But others require a much more relative judgment. Fantasy in particular is a stumbling block. Is fantasy a genre on its own, or does it include a number of genres, such as the horror film, the fairy tale, science fiction, allegory, the musical? For that matter, are any of these possible sub-genres necessarily fantastic? Is fantasy defined by its subject matter, or its treatment, or a bit of both? Can one man's fantasy be another's hard reality? Is a film such as *The Exorcist* a fantasy or not? Its treatment is firmly realistic, but its supernatural subject matter will place it at once in the realm of fantasy for most

people. And yet almost anyone subscribing to Christian belief in one form or another is required to accept the possibility of demonic possession as an objective reality; if one does so believe, then surely there is nothing at all fantastic about the film. Similarly, fantasy may be closely connected with one's place in time. *Destination Moon* may have seemed an out-and-out fantasy in 1950, whereas now, with hindsight, its depiction of man's first steps on the moon looks like the soberest documentary.

The argument can go on forever. The Structuralist critic Tzvetan Todorov, for example, goes so far as to define two categories: the uncanny (that which seems to be supernatural, but finally proves susceptible of explanation according to known natural laws) and the marvellous (that which is governed by laws unknown to us and requires some modification of our ideas of the world around us); the fantastic, he says, is the duration of our uncertainty between these two choices. By this standard, I suppose, *The Turn of the Screw* would be an ideal example of the sustained fantastic, since we can never certainly decide whether the governess' experiences are uncanny (she is having delusions) or marvellous (the ghosts really exist), but either way we have to bend language somewhat to redefine two words just in order to define a third in relation to them.

Wisely, it seems to me, Charles Derry elects to sidestep this rather fruitless area of controversy. The area he is dealing with, the horror film, is ambiguously related to fantasy. According to Todorov's formulation, it may contain the uncanny, the marvellous, and the fantastic; it may also contain none of them. It also has a considerable area of overlap with science fiction, though stalwart attempts have been made to insist on the separateness of the two genres. What has been sorely needed in studies of the horror film genre is some sort of pattern which would enable us to fit everything we vaguely feel to belong to the genre into a sensible definition without either straining the definition or distorting the individual examples. This Charles Derry provides through a detailed study of the horror film in the 1960s and 1970s, examined mainly in terms of how they direct their audiences' responses, what the prime sources of horror in them are.

These sources Derry categorizes into three broad types: horror of personality, horror of Armageddon, and horror of the demonic. Without compromising too much his complex and subtle arguments, one may point out that the first category comfortably contains a lot of psychological thrillers and dark dramas (as well as some black comedies) in which there is no question of possible supernatural participation, but in which the chills come from the uncharted depths of the human psyche (the menace is within us). The second category is mainly occupied by the more frightening (though not necessarily the more fantastic) areas of science fiction, in which the horror derives from some outside threat to humanity and the world as we know it. And the third, the only one which directly involves the supernatural, gathers up all those films which concern themselves with the workings of some malign non-human force aiming at a revolution of evil through a radical reshaping of human personality, individually or collectively.

What all of these have in common is that they present varied facets of the same malevolent universe. Man is threatened from within and without. He cannot fathom his own nature, he cannot be sure the birds and beasts will not turn on him, the earth split open or burst into flames, or creatures from another planet come and deprive him of his birthright; he may doubt, but how can he ever know for certain, that the dark gods are dead; that a personal devil may impregnate his wife or transform his child into a monster. Horror is insecurity, horror is uncertainty; and horror is also the dawning conviction that our worst fears cannot hold a candle to the enormity of the reality they half reveal, half conceal from us. Horror films are distinguished as a genre by the stratagems they use on us to make us explore our own fears, to force us to consider the possibility that bad as we think things are, they are probably in actuality a lot worse.

Given this emphasis in Derry's definition of the horror genre on the ways an audience's responses can be manipulated, it is hardly surprising that Hitchcock should occupy such an obviously key position in his argument. For of Hitchcock above all other film-makers it has been said that he directs the audience much more than he directs the film. I once ran into some argument over my inclusion of Hitchcock in a book subtitled "Some Key Film-Makers of the Sixties." But the seminal role played by *Psycho* in the development of "horror of personality" and by *The Birds* in "horror of Armageddon," both of them important sub-genres belonging specifically to the 1960s, would seem to bear out the contention. It is curious, though, that Hitchcock, a devout Catholic from childhood, should not have touched the third type, "horror of the demonic," and has had virtually no truck with the supernatural at all in his career. Does it perhaps come too close to home for a true believer? Who knows?

But the fact remains that Hitchcock, an unarguable auteur if there ever was one, here plays a vital role in the definition of a genre. One wonders, when Hitchcock these days speaks of doing a chase in a certain way just because it is always done another way, just how clearly he realizes that it is always done that way largely because he himself set the convention. Whether he does realize this or not, he clearly lives at the point where auteur criticism and genre criticism join hands, since the great individual creates or re-creates the genre, and then is influenced by it in his subsequent practice just as much as anyone else, as though the conventions have become a fact of life. This is just one of the fascinating lines of thought *Dark Dreams* leads us to. Maybe in a later book Charles Derry will be moved to pursue them further himself, building on his own original insights which are so plentifully in evidence here.

John Russell Taylor

ACKNOWLEDGMENTS

The author would like to thank Stuart Kaminsky for his encouragement and friendship; the Northwestern University Film Faculty for their part in instilling in the author an approach to film study; the gracious and generous John Russell Taylor for his Foreword; Frederick S. Clarke of *Cinefantastique* for the use of his stills and the permission to republish material originally appearing in his excellent magazine; and Dan R. Scapperotti, Dale Winogura, Tony Scott, and Bill Crouch for the interview material on William Castle, Curtis Harrington, George Romero, and William Friedkin respectively.

5110-30

Introduction

In 1960 when I was nine years old I remember very vividly dragging my reluctant parents to see Alfred Hitchcock's *Psycho*. My parents were afraid it might horrify me, but as I tried to reassure them, *that* was the whole point of going—and besides, I had it on the very good authority of the seven-year-old girl across the street that the movie had only two or three really scary parts anyway. The film was shown at the Southgate Cinema in Maple Heights, Ohio, one of the first suburban movie theaters to be located in the middle of a huge shopping center. Unlike the old theaters, the seats of the Cinema had an upright and a reclining position; how scary the movie was could be judged by how often the pressure of your feet against the floor pushed the seat back to its uncomfortable, upright position. Throughout *Psycho*, the noise of the seats—at that time still a novelty—was often louder than Bernard Herrmann's strings. I remember being enthralled when during the brutal shower murder the entire audience screamed in unison. Why did they scream? And how was it that a film that was supposed to horrify could at the same time be so entertaining—or were all of us masochists? Indeed, what *was* the nature of the relationship between this horror film and its audience? And why in 1960 were we all trooping off to see *Psycho* and not a sequel to *Frankenstein?* The purpose of this study is to explore these questions, and while doing so to provide a history of the three new subgenres of horror film, which emerged during the 1960s.

DARK DREAMS

"We all go a little mad sometimes."
—Anthony Perkins in *Psycho*

"So you met someone
and now you know how it feels,
Goody, goody.
Hooray and Hallelujah,
you had it comin' to ya.
Goody, goody for you.
Goody, goody for me.
I hope you're satisfied,
you rascal, you."
—"Goody, Goody" from
What's the Matter with Helen?

Not Bram Stoker or Mary Shelley,
But Robert Bloch, Boileau-Narcejac
    and Henry Farrell.

Not Vincent Price, Boris Karloff,
    or Bela Lugosi,
But Bette Davis, Anthony Perkins,
    Joan Crawford, and Shelley
    Winters.

"This long disease, my life . . ."
—Mary Astor in
Hush, Hush, Sweet Charlotte

1

THE HORROR OF PERSONALITY

Did the horror film die in the fifties and early sixties? Although a good case could be made for the answer yes, it is probably more accurate to suggest that the classic horror film, like *Frankenstein, Dracula,* or *King Kong*, had been supplanted in the fifties by the science-fiction horror film, which was a logical outgrowth of the end-of-the-war, atomic-bomb anxieties. When the horror film returned in the sixties without the science-fiction paraphernalia of spaceships and interplanetary monsters, the traditional horror genre had been transformed largely into one of three new subgenres—the first and most important of which I call the "horror of personality." In order to understand exactly what the horror of personality entailed and exactly why it managed to become the dominant force in box-office horror in the early sixties, one must first understand the horror traditions from which this subgenre began to break.

One of the most important aspects of the classic horror film is the physical form of the horror itself. Usually the form (in other words, the monster) is something abstracted from man: a horror that keeps its distance from man both aesthetically and metaphysically. For instance, Dracula is physically unlike the average man in his dress, his fangs, and his behavior; although any man may become a vampire, the world can quite visibly be divided into vampires and nonvampires. King Kong is also quite physically unlike man: he is gigantic and an ape. Quite obviously these monsters are horrible because they present alternatives to the tenuous human equilibrium; that is, a vampire is too close to man for comfort; even on a simplistic level it is

obvious that King Kong represents an aspect of man that man has managed to suppress. As presented in the classic horror story, the horror itself is both distanced from man and, what is more important, highly symbolic. The horror may be a metaphorical manifestation of man's animal instincts *(King Kong)*, his evil desires (witches, Satanism), or his fear of being dead yet not at rest *(The Mummy,* zombies); but the horror is certainly not man itself. This separation usually enables man in the horror films to confront directly his evil enemy as surely as one could confront one's reflection in a distorted mirror. Almost always the horror is vanquished.

An interesting variation of this pattern, and one that by contrast makes the symbolic schizophrenia in the usual classic horror film even more clear, is the *Doctor Jekyll and Mr. Hyde* series, in which the normal man and the horror actually coexist in the same body. This lessening of the aesthetic and metaphysical distances between the horror and man makes the *Jekyll-Hyde* series an interesting precursor to the horror-of-personality film; for in the Stevenson series the horror is already less symbolic and, indeed, quite literal: a struggle between man's rational and animal instincts. The horror-of-personality films in the sixties, such as *Psycho, Strait-Jacket,* and *What Ever Happened to Baby Jane?*, decrease the distance of the horror even further. The horror becomes not at all symbolic, but quite specific.

Aside from studying the nature of the horror, it is equally important to study the explanation of the horror within the context of the story. In the classic horror story, there are two basic methods of explaining things away—either supernaturally or pseudoscientifically. Into the supernatural group one could fit all the monsters and horrors that are somehow involved with religions and ritual. This would include all the witchcraft movies (with their obvious Christian basis) and other horrors, such as *The Mummy* (Egyptology and reincarnation), *Dracula* (Christianity, again), zombie movies (with their stress on voodoo), and perhaps even *The Golem* (with its magic book and magic star). Into the other, the pseudoscientific group, one could fit all the monsters and horrors that are the result of a scientist character who goes too far. This group would include the *Wolf Man*, all the animal men, and, of course, all the *Frankenstein* variations. An interesting variation of the mad-scientist explanation is used in *King Kong*, where the mad scientist is represented by the "mad" movie director who quite literally goes too far; that is, back to a prehistoric island.

Historically, the pseudoscientific basis proved to be more fruitful during the fifties. It was during this period that the science-fiction genre became important, helping both to blur the distinctions between the two genres and seemingly to end temporarily the popularity of the supernatural basis—at least until the very personal Roger Corman cycle in the early sixties, and the striking reemergence of the witchcraft cycle in the late sixties. It is quite important to notice that in movies such as *Psycho*, *What Ever Happened to Baby Jane?*, *Hush, Hush, Sweet Charlotte*, *Lady in a Cage*, and *Peeping Tom* the extreme specificity of the horror, and the horror's manifestation as insanity, make both of the two classic bases for explanation unnecessary. Can *Psycho* be explained away either supernaturally or pseudoscientifically? Quite clearly, the terms are not only unnecessary, but inapplicable. It was in the early sixties, during the Kennedy years, that the country began to be racked by violence. Crime began to go up astronomically, and suddenly there were riots in the streets, which the people could just not understand. And perhaps even more importantly, senseless mass murderers (Richard Speck, the Boston Strangler, Charles Whitman, etc.) were constantly in the headlines. (Indeed, it is interesting to note that the highest concentration numerically of these films took place in 1964–1965, directly after the Kennedy assassination.) Thus, in this period, one can see why pseudoscientific horror or supernatural horror were not really the concerns of the

day. What *was* horrible, however, was man. It was a horror that was specific, nonabstract, and one that did not need a metaphor. Since the symbolic schizophrenia of the classic horror film had now become a literal insanity, it was necessary for a whole new basis of explanation to be applied. What does seem to have been adopted in the early sixties in these horror films (however sometimes skeptically) was the psychological explanation. Violence and horror were not explained in terms of science or religion, but in terms of psychology. This is made obvious by the end of *Psycho*, the very Freudian-recurring Oedipal complexes (in especially the Aldrich films), and the obsession with sex in all the films from *Psycho* to *Strait-Jacket* to *Berserk* to *Mania* to *Orgasmo*. In a way, the psychological explanation enables us to distance ourselves from the horror: "It's all right, it was something in his mind that made the killer sick." It's really amazing to notice how often in these films the Freudian explanation seems to make almost no sense, yet the viewers, willing to grasp onto anything in order to alleviate their own fears, will quickly accept it. How many people have come out of *Psycho* reassured, saying: "It was about a crazy man who thought he was his mother"; rather than: "It was about a man who seemed to be just about as normal as you or me, but really wasn't." It is not until the end of the sixties that the psychological base also begins to be rejected overtly. *The Devil's Own* in 1967 and especially *Rosemary's Baby* in 1968 mark the reemergence of the supernatural as a major force in explaining away evil; and *Targets* and *Pretty Poison* in 1968 both exhibit a strange kind of matter-of-factness to their violence, which suggests that—and this perhaps is the most horrible of all—*there is no explanation*: some people just kill.[1]

Before I go on and discuss what may be a waning of the horror-of-personality films as a distinct and thriving subgenre, it would now be fruitful to discuss the films in question, concentrating not only on the strict horror-of-personality films, but also on those outside the (sub)genre that in some way relate to the genre's development or refinement. Certainly the one group of films that had a tremendous

[1]It is interesting to note that, although Hitchcock also pioneered in the second subgenre of horror—the horror of Armageddon—when he made *The Birds* in 1962, this subgenre of outside forces taking over the world with no pseudoscientific, religious, or psychological explanation acceptable did not really thrive until roughly the late sixties and early seventies (*Willard, Ben, Frogs, Night of the Lepus*, etc.)—the same period as these later matter-of-fact-horror-of-personality films.

Elizabeth Dear witnesses the stabbing of her father by her mother (Isla Cameron) in *Nightmare*: psychology of violence

developmental influence on the horror-of-personality films were the *films noirs* of the forties: Siodmak films like *Phantom Lady* (1944), *Uncle Harry* (1946), *The Dark Mirror* (1946), and *The Spiral Staircase* (1946); and Lang films like *The Woman in the Window* (1944), *Scarlet Street* (1945), and *The Secret Beyond the Door* (1948). These *films noirs*, with their atmospheric lighting, their strong relation to German expressionism, and their preoccupation with disintegration, madness, and decay, come very close to the horror of personality. So do many of the Hitchcock thrillers of the forties dealing with psychopathology, such as *Suspicion* (1941), *Shadow of a Doubt* (1943), *Spellbound* (1945), and especially *Strangers on a Train* (1951). If some of these Hitchcock films are a bit too cheerful in their development and sunny in their denouement to

come across with the sensibility of the horror genre, they augur nevertheless to the two films I consider seminal to the genre: *Diabolique* and *Psycho*.

Diabolique was made in 1955, and its inclusion as a seminal film may seem initially surprising. First of all, the film does not come out of the horror tradition as much as it comes out of the tightly constructed, suspense-melodrama *oeuvre* of its director, Henri-Georges Clouzot. And, secondly, the film predates the cycle of the true horror-of-personality films by at least five years. Nevertheless, the film is responsible for delineating many of the horror elements that would later become so dominant in the genre. The plot, based on the novel by Boileau and Narcejac (the same team that wrote the novel on which Hitchcock's 1958 pre-*Psycho* exercise in psychopathology *Vertigo* was based), is very complex; at its center is the rather strange and almost perverse relationships between two women played by Simone Signoret·and Vera Clouzot, two women

19

Diabolique: Vera Clouzot recoils in horror

Diabolique: Will the children find the corpse?

who are inextricably entangled in a monstrous crime: the murder of the one woman's husband. At the end of the film it is discovered that the plot is even more complicated than originally thought, and that the unmarried woman had plotted with the husband all along (who was really not killed), and was trying rather to drive the other woman crazy. Of course the plot idea of trying to drive someone crazy in not completely new; Charles Boyer tried to do it to Ingrid Bergman in *Gaslight* in 1944, but in that film (and those of that type) the emphasis was on the mysterious elements belonging more to the Daphne du Maurier or Mary Stewart Gothic Romance. In *Diabolique*, the emphasis is on the rather everyday, matter-of-fact, sordid horror, and on the tense psychological relationships between the characters. The subject matter of *Diabolique*, that of two women in a psychological horrific situation, can be seen in many of the notable horror-of-personality

Diabolique: Two woman (Simone Signoret and Vera Clouzot) psychologically bound

films of the sixties—most specifically: *What Ever Happened to Baby Jane?*, *Nightmare*, *Hush, Hush, Sweet Charlotte*, *Picture Mommy Dead*, *Games*, *The Mad Room*, *What Ever Happened to Aunt Alice?*, and *What's the Matter with Helen?* Of course the Clouzot film does not quite have the same poetically pessimistic quality of some of the later films, in that its action is surprisingly void of sad, poignant time jumps; in that the relative youth of its women deprives the film of a particular pathos. The film also lacks the very strong emphasis on insanity itself, which was, with *Psycho* in 1960, to become perhaps the strongest of the genre's traits. The film does, however, contain strong elements of the ambiguity that later was to become such an important part: the unanglicized title of the film is *Les Diaboliques*, or *The Fiends*. While watching the film, one assumes that the fiends are Simone Signoret and Vera

Clouzot; at its end one presumes the true fiends are Simone Signoret and Paul Meurisse. The question to be asked is: "Who, then, are the true *Diaboliques*? Or are we all fiends?" In the sixties, with *Psycho* and *Hush, Hush, Sweet Charlotte*, we are to ask a similar question, but with a different object: "Who, then, are the true crazy people? Or are we all?"

Except perhaps for *Screaming Mimi* (a film made in 1958 that contains many of the same ideas as *Psycho* but in a less-integrated form), *Psycho* marks the true beginning of the horror-of-personality genre. It is a seminal film not only because of its emphasis on the ambiguity and horror of insanity, but also because it was tremendously successful in terms of its box-office. It was evidently dealing with issues to which the audiences were responding, and it, almost single-handedly, managed to spawn the genre. I will not try to deal with the film in terms of Hitchcock as *auteur* (as it has been done quite

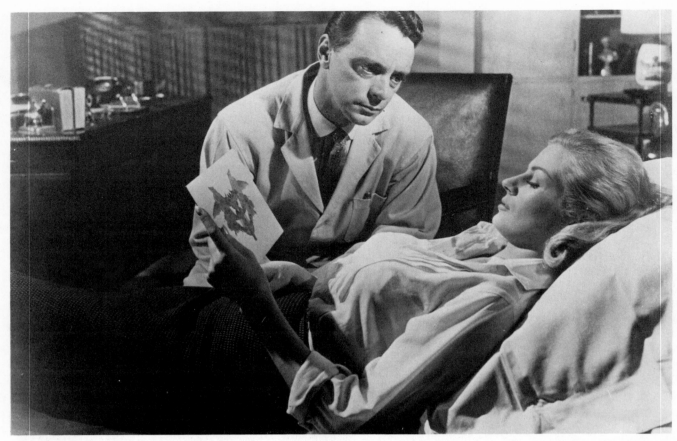

Anita Ekberg and Harry Townes in *Screaming Mimi*: the recurrence of psychoanalysis

admirably by such as Robin Wood and V.F. Perkins), but, instead, will deal with the film in terms of the genre it was breaking away from, a manner in which I believe the film has rarely been discussed. As I stated before, the classic pseudo-scientific horror film was changed in the fifties to the dominant science-fiction film, or the science-fiction horror. The supernatural horror film seemed to become relatively recessive during the fifties, although the ~~supernatural~~ supernatural tradition was carried on rather strangely by a series of haunted-house movies in the late fifties. In fact, during the period between *Diabolique* in 1955 and *Psycho* in 1960, these haunted-house movies were the dominant element (in terms of number of films released) in the supernatural horror; although of course these films were, by and large, continuations of the grade-B haunted-house films that were such a staple in the forties. Some of the titles in these fifties films include *The Screaming Skull* (1958), *House on Haunted Hill* (1958), *Horrors of the Black Museum* (1959), *The Bat* (1959), *Terror in the Haunted House*

House on Haunted Hill: Vincent Price as horror master of ceremonies

22

(1958), *I Bury the Living* (1958), and *13 Ghosts* (1960). Many of these films were William Castle Productions or for American International. Even more featured some special kind of gimmick, such as *Macabre*, where theatre patrons received a thousand-dollar life-insurance policy from Lloyds of London in case any of them should die of fright; or "Emergo" (in *House on Haunted Hill*), where a wired skeleton would float over the heads of the audience; or "PsychoRama" (in *Terror in the Haunted House*), in which subliminal pictures were used to psychologically affect the audience; or "Percepto" (in *The Tingler*), where vibrating motors were attached to the underside of theatre seats, which at the proper moments caused tingling sensations in a delicate portion of the theatregoer's anatomy; or "Hypnomagic" (in *The Hypnotic Eye*), in which one of the actors tries to hypnotize the audience; or "Illusion-O" (in *13 Ghosts*), in which special glasses allow the ghosts to become visible to the audience. Not all of these movies took place in haunted houses (*I Bury the Living* took place in a graveyard); nevertheless, the idea of horror in these films was very clearly associated with a dark environment. And in almost all of these movies the horror was experienced by the audience as supernatural and mystical: in *House on Haunted Hill*, there are scary apparitions; in *I Bury the Living*, people who own funeral plots begin dying as a psychic result of the cemetery owner's error of mixing up the plots on his map. Yet ironically enough, although the shocks in these films are largely experienced as horror, the denouement of the films suggests that the films are really in the mystery genre and are only masquerading as horror. For instance, in *House on Haunted Hill* we discover that all the apparitions have only been carefully sustained illusions carried out by Vincent Price; and in *I Bury the Living* we discover that the people have really been killed by a gravedigger who, being phased out of his job, wanted revenge. Thus in both of these films, the horror of the supernatural, in terms of the plot itself, did not really ever exist in the first place. Perhaps this tradition can be traced back to that famous theatre and film staple, *Seven Keys to*

Movie patron is tingled in *The Tingler*

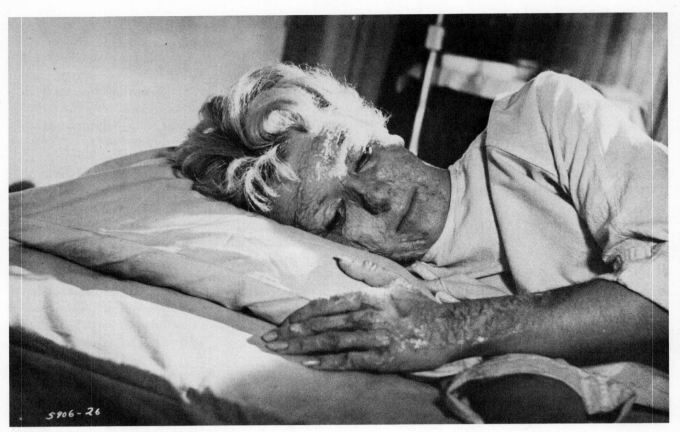

The Hypnotic Eye: face of horror

Baldpate, and also (though less directly) to those mystery novels that proliferated in the twenties and thirties in which, one by one, people in a haunted house/island/ski lodge/etc. are killed; except that in the haunted-house films, the horror-mystical elements are played up and the rational explain-it-all denouements are played down. *Psycho*, quite apart from any *auteur* considerations, can be seen to relate quite clearly to this spate of haunted-house movies—most obviously, since the main house in *Psycho* is absolutely typical with its stairways, dark corners, and hidden basement. Yet the most amazing thing about *Psycho* is that from the beginning to the end it very consciously goes against all the established conventions, and in doing so manages to redefine exactly what horror is by relating it to the modern 1960s sensibilities. For instance, although the major horror in the haunted-house movies takes place in the dark of the house, *Psycho*'s major horror takes place in the bright whiteness of a shower stall. Hitchcock uses the very generic house in his film only to foil the audience's expectations of having the most horrific act happen there. And, when Hitchcock finally does use the house as the

environment of horror (when Arbogast is killed), the horror does not proceed from the house itself; rather, it proceeds from the character of the killer for which the house is only a metaphor. And whereas many of the haunted-house films are really mystery films masquerading as horror, *Psycho*, with its inquiring detective, is really a horror film masquerading as a mystery. (After all, Hitchcock even murders the detective.) Although in many of the haunted-house movies the explanation at the end alleviates, or actually repudiates, the earlier horror, the explanation and denouement at the end of *Psycho* tend to crystallize the horror even further. In regard to the classic horror genre, *Psycho* also breaks away, in that the fear in *Psycho* is not particularly of death or symbolic evil; the fear is instead of living in a crazy world, a world in which one can be mutilated physically in close-up. As such, *Psycho* takes what had been a minor theme from the mad-scientist films—insanity—and augments its horror by using it completely unrelated to any mystic-scientific superpositions, such as a Frankenstein monster or a Wolf Man. Thus, the film breaks away from the two standard realms of horror—the pseudoscientific and the supernatural—and substi-

Anthony Perkins and the archetypal old, dark house in *Psycho*

Janet Leigh and John Gavin in *Psycho:* sexual identities

tutes instead the psychological. Indeed, in its redefinition of horror as the psychological, a step that seemed in 1960 (five years after *Diabolique*) particularly suited to the times, in its concern with the anxiety of living and the nearness of multilation, and most especially in its emphasis on the ambiguity of insanity ("We all go a little mad sometime," says Anthony Perkins), *Psycho* can be viewed as the fountainhead from which all the horror-of-personality films were to flow.

Right after *Psycho* began breaking box-office records, the Louis Malle film, *Elevator to the Scaffold*, was released in the United States with the changed title *Frantic*, probably to try to cash in a bit on *Psycho*'s success. *Frantic* was followed by the William Castle production of *Homicidal*. *Homicidal* is about Miriam Webster's relationship with her half-brother Warren and his strange wife Emily. At the end of the film, after some killings (the knife again being the horrible and phallic weapon), it is discovered that Warren and Emily are one and the same person. Although I have never been able to follow completely the explanation at the end (I'm still not sure whether Warren/Emily was at birth a boy or a girl), it is quite clear that transvestism, sexual perversion, and perhaps even an operation in Denmark were involved in his/her horrible identity. The confusion is further compounded by a literal double curtain call at the film's end in which the star's name is revealed as Jean (Gene?) Arless, without the slightest clue as to whether he/she was in real life a man or a woman. The effect is really quite unsettling. It may be possible that Jean Arless' nonappearance in film thereafter may be related to the ambiguity of her sexuality. Ironically, before the ending of the film both Warren and Emily appear to by physically, normally good-looking; after the surprise is revealed, they are both perceived by the audience as looking rather bizarre. *Homicidal* is basically important for its reassociation of insanity with sexuality. It is a relationship that is reaffirmed in many of the films—especially those of the early sixties, such as *Peeping Tom, The Psychopath, The Collector, Hush, Hush, Sweet Charlotte, Die, Die, My Darling,* and *Twisted Nerve.* Indeed, the element of sexual perversion, or at least of sexuality off-kilter (such as in *What Ever Happened to Baby Jane?*), is present in many of the films even when it is not related directly to the possible insanity of the protagonists. The influence of *Psycho* is further and quite obviously apparent in many of the titles released in the sixties—titles that include *Mania, Trauma, Maniac, Dementia 13, Strait-Jacket, Pyro, Shock Treatment, The Psychopath, Psycho-Circus, Berserk, Twisted Nerve, The Mad Room, Fanatic* (the alternate title of *Die, Die, My Darling*), and even *Paranoia* (an Italian sexploitation film originally called *Orgasmo,* but partially an homage to Aldrich's two horror films).

The next really important film in the horror-of-personality genre is *What Ever Happened to Baby Jane?*, made in 1962. This film, as was its companion piece, *Hush, Hush, Sweet Charlotte,* was directed by Robert Aldrich. The reviews of *Baby Jane* were on the whole much better than those of *Sweet Charlotte;* but even in the laudable reviews, there was a general tendency to dismiss the films as only horror films—as *grand guignol*—as if a horror film could not be worth serious consideration. Actually, the contribution of Robert Aldrich to the horror-of-personality films cannot be overestimated. There arises here the question of *auteur* vs. genre: It seems to me that while Aldrich is most probably an *auteur,* it is equally obvious that he is an *auteur* working

within and against certain genre conventions (just as Curtis Harrington was to do later in *Games* and *What's the Matter with Helen?*). It does not seem that these two approaches—*auteur* and genre—need to be necessarily antagonistic. The reason Aldrich was so important to the development of the genre is because it was he and his scriptwriter, Lukas Heller (and of course the novelist Henry Farrell), who realized the relevance of *Diabolique,* and in *What Ever Happened to Baby Jane?* joined the major ideas of *Diabolique* and *Psycho.* What emerged then was a psychological study of two women whose relationship was based on some past crime, yet a study that dealt very overtly with the ambiguity of insanity. After combining these two basic premises, Aldrich went on to invent more or less his own conventions; conventions that he would follow very carefully in his next film, and conventions that would be followed just as carefully in some of the Curtis Harrington films years later. (Why is it that when Greek tragedy follows conventions and repeats itself it is intellectual; but when a horror film follows conventions it is too often regarded as clichéd repetition?) The first major element that Aldrich added is his use of the audience's awareness of his actors. In his films he cast aging movie stars. The sight of a bizarre Bette Davis making her comeback by torturing Joan Crawford, whom she has always disliked, adds an extra dimension to *Baby Jane* that fits right in with its tone: a poignancy, mixed with voyeurism and revulsion. In *Hush, Hush, Sweet Charlotte* Aldrich goes even further: he uses four aging actresses—Olivia de Havilland, Bette Davis, Agnes Moorehead, and Mary Astor. Particularly effective is Mary Astor: although the audience may remember her as the beautiful girl in *The Maltese Falcon,* all the audience sees is a bloated, wrinkled, pale woman who is half dead when she first appears. Surely this cannot be the Mary Astor we once knew so well. But, of course, time stops for no one, and everyone must get old and, so it seems, ugly. In each film Aldrich also casts Victor Buono—certainly a rather bizarre actor. In the first film he plays a grotesque mamma's boy, and in the second, father to the grotesque pappa's girl. Perhaps the most important difference between *Diabolique* and the Aldrich films is the distance Aldrich puts between the main crime and his story. In *Diabolique* the narrative was structurally simpler: a crime was committed (supposedly), and the story proceeded immediately from there. In both

26

Julie Harris in *The Haunting*: an archetypal haunted house.

Peeping Tom: voyeurism and sexuality

Homicidal: Patricia Breslin and Jean Arless (right, as Warren) in her male identity.

Victor Buono and Bette Davis in *What Ever Happened to Baby Jane?*

Baby Jane and *Sweet Charlotte*, a crime is committed, and then the narrative jumps ahead about thirty years to continue the story. And this jump is not merely a structural maneuver, but also a thematic one; while the tragedy of *Diabolique* is a specific one and of a specific time, the tragedy of the Aldrich films includes the horror of completely wasted lives. Although *Baby Jane* and *Sweet Charlotte* work within Aldrich's very tight framework much like a musical theme and variation, each film is a remarkably integrated work unto itself.

The first thing we hear in *What Ever Happened to Baby Jane?* is a girl crying and a voice saying: "Want to see it again little girl? It shouldn't frighten you." The sound of tears, the immediate suggestion that *Baby Jane* will be a tragedy, is particularly apt. We are then introduced to the two sisters, Blanche and Jane. From the very beginning, the little girl Jane (the Bette Davis character) is flamboyant, while Blanche (the Joan Crawford character) is sullen. The highlight of the 1917 episode is a closeup of the Joan Crawford character as her mother tells her: "You're the lucky one, Blanche. Someday you'll be the famous one . . . and you can treat your sister kinder than she's been treating you." And then from Blanche, very coldly: "I won't forget." We skip to the year 1935. The roles have been reversed, and Joan Crawford is the famous actress, Bette Davis the untalented sister. Yet it appears that Joan Crawford is treating her sister very kindly and exerting her influence to get Bette Davis some parts. However, Aldrich inserts touches that in retrospect suggest the true nature of Joan Crawford. When a studio

executive walks past Crawford's big car, he asks, "What do they make monsters like this for?" And the answer is: "For Blanche Hudson." And not: "For Baby Jane." Thus, Joan Crawford is very clearly equated with a monster. The climax of the precredit sequence is the very confusing presentation of the accident. We see closeups of feet, of a light dress against a fence, of a hand shifting gears, then a crash. Later we are to take it for granted that Bette Davis ran over Joan Crawford, thus causing her paralysis. Yet what image does Aldrich provide us with as a metaphor for the accident?: a Baby Jane doll with its head crushed. And indeed, it is Baby Jane (who always dresses in light colors) who is the victim. In retrospect it is amazing how many clues Aldrich provides us with which we go right ahead and ignore. Finally we get to the credits, and then the bulk of the story starts with the title "Yesterday." We are prepared for the introduction of the aged Joan Crawford and Bette Davis by first watching the neighbors discuss them while watching an old Blanche Hudson movie (Joan Crawford in *Sadie McKee*, 1934). Although *Baby Jane* is unlike both *Psycho* and *Diabolique* in that the crime does not seem to have been sexually related, there is a remarkable emphasis on off-balance sexuality. The neighbors, played by Anna Lee and Bette Davis' real-life daughter, are never shown with men; neither is Joan Crawford. The only suggestion of a relationship is that between Bette Davis and Victor Buono, but it is presented as a gross parody, a grotesque. (Note that in *Hush, Hush, Sweet Charlotte* that element is provided by Cecil Kellaway, and it becomes, unlike in *Baby Jane*, affirming.) And indeed, our first view of Victor Buono standing with his tiny possessive mother suggests the Diane Arbus of the seventies. Certainly the relationship between these two is not normal. Notice too the homage to the seminal film *Psycho*, in that the name of the neighbor is the same as Anthony Perkins' mysterious mother: Mrs. Bates.

Although the basic situation of the story seems to be that Bette Davis is the crazy and evil sister, and Joan Crawford the suffering, good, and sane sister, Aldrich constantly includes details that foreshadow the ending and that suggest otherwise. Our first view of the aged Joan Crawford is that of her kindly sweet face suddenly becoming harsh as she criticizes an old movie director. Suggestively, it is Bette Davis who wears light colors, and Joan Crawford who wears black. For someone who is supposed to be crazy and evil, Bette Davis shows remarkable intelligence. She realizes that Joan Crawford called the business manager and accuses her rightly of lying to her: "You're just a liar. You always were." The revelation that Bette Davis' whole life was wasted because of Joan Crawford's lying adds particular irony to her accurate accusation. Not only is Bette Davis intelligent, but she has a sense of humor that truly draws us toward her. "It's not me that needs a doctor, Blanche . . ." says Davis; or after particularly frightening her sister: "You're just a neurotic." And there is the whole business of the surprise dinner with the dead rat, which, although horrible, shows amazing creativity. The innuendo, "By the way, Blanche, there's rats in the cellar," is hilarious. Funny too is her baby-talk explanation: "I didn't forget your breakfast . . . I didn't bring your breakfast . . . because you didn't eat your din-din." Joan Crawford, on the other hand, seems amazingly devoid of either wit or a sense of humor. But, after all, she is the dark sister. The basic crisis in *Baby Jane* (just as it is in *Sweet Charlotte*) is the question of the house. Since it was built for Baby Jane by her father, she doesn't want to leave it. (And, in *Sweet Charlotte*, the house is again identified with the father figure.) In the Aldrich films, the house is used very differently from the way it is used in some of the haunted-house films. In some haunted-house films, a girl is often tormented by nightmares and memories that she cannot exorcise until she returns to the house. In both *Baby Jane* and *Sweet Charlotte*, it is quite clear that Bette Davis cannot exorcise her demons until she goes away from the house. Perversely, in both films Bette Davis wants to stay. Another important element that recurs in most of the films from *Diabolique* to *Psycho* to *Sweet Charlotte* to *Pretty Poison* is the disposal-of-the-body sequence, although in *Baby Jane* there is a nice initial ambiguity as to whether Bette Davis is disposing a body or her black-shrouded sister. It is not until the end of the film and outside the house in the light of a sunny beach that Joan Crawford finally tells Bette Davis the truth: Crawford's paralysis resulted when Crawford tried to cripple Davis. After a life of self-torture and unnecessary guilt, Davis answers with a compassion that is horrifying: "You mean, all this time we could have been friends?" She goes off to try to rekindle the friendship by buying ice-cream cones (and it was an ice-cream cone she wanted in the precredit 1917 sequence.) Almost magically, the grotesque makeup and wrink-

les disappear from her face. She becomes truly beautiful; and with the guilt no longer heavy on her shoulders, her movements are light. Ironically, in her salvation she reverts back to her childhood. Yet, as Davis sheds guilt and years, Crawford takes them on. The movie ends with Bette Davis dancing a dance of liberation as she approaches that black, corpselike figure, which is Joan Crawford. Despite the relatively "happy ending," it is too late for the revelation to really matter. If only it had come decades sooner! The two sisters' lives have already been wasted; there is really no time left to make of them anything meaningful or worthwhile.

Hush, Hush, Sweet Charlotte was made by Aldrich in 1964 and written by the same group of writers—Lukas Heller and Henry Farrell; and were it not for Joan Crawford's illness, Bette Davis would have again played opposite her. As it turned out, Olivia de Havilland stepped in and took Crawford's part. *Sweet Charlotte*, like *Baby Jane*, starts in the past. The year is 1927, and almost immediately we get the strong father figure, played by Victor Buono. Even the father's portrait towers over the John Mayhew character. In this remarkably integrated film, one of the first icons we notice is a painting on a wall: Charlotte, her father, and probably her cousin—except that Charlotte and her father are painted in bright shades that attract the eye, while the other girl is in dark shades that recede into the background. Thus the two girls' relationship should be discernible quite early. The crime, this time very overtly related to sexuality, is again handled in confusing and horrifying closeups. The decapitation and the severing of the hand are clearly substitutions for castration. Immediately after the killing Aldrich cuts to the bandleader who yells out "One more time." His remark may seem at first only terribly heavy-handed black comedy, but actually it is quite a foreshadowing device; before Charlotte can be "cured" she will have to go through the experience at least one more time. In many respects this suggests a clear relationship between these two Aldrich films and Hitchcock's *Marnie*. In *Marnie*, the heroine was forced to reenact the crime (through the symbolic shooting of her horse Forio); only then could she leave the house of her mother with no guilt. The same thing holds true in Aldrich's films. In *Baby Jane*, Jane cannot leave the house until she really has "tortured" her sister, as she supposedly had in the past. The parallel is even stronger in *Sweet Charlotte* (in fact, the John Mayhew character

Two adversaries, representing past and present, confront each other in *Hush, Hush, Sweet Charlotte*: Bette Davis and Olivia de Havilland

whose death causes Charlotte's madness is played by the parallel sailor in *Marnie*, Bruce Dern). Before Charlotte can leave the house of her father, she must go through the experience of reenacting the crime in the dream sequence and "shooting" Joseph Cotten. Yet the difference in attitude between *Marnie* and the Aldrich films show why *Marnie* is not a horror film: Marnie is really guilty of the past crime and is cured while she is relatively young. Baby Jane and Charlotte are not guilty, and they are not cured of their madness until their whole lives have been wasted and it is too late. After the crime (the killing of Mayhew), the story jumps to 1964. Immediately, the problem of moving out of the house is made clear: Bette Davis pushes a gigantic flower pot off the second-floor balcony in an attempt to stop the bulldozers from razing her house. (At the end of the

film, she will, quite symetrically, push the second and final flower pot off the porch in order to execute de Havilland and Cotten.) The house is again bizarrely stopped in time; the Southern gentility of 1927 now appears faded, run-down, but unchanged. When Olivia de Havilland first arrives she says: "It's just as I left it." And that was thirty-seven years ago. Ironically, Bette Davis had always wanted to play the archetypal Southern belle, Scarlett O'Hara. Now, in 1964, she manages to do just that—but decades too late; her Charlotte-Scarlett is a pathetic creature to behold. Out of place, out of time, she wears clothes from 1927, and even treats her best friend, Velma, the maid, with a particularly Southern *noblesse oblige*. The contrast between the two cousins is obvious, for de Havilland has changed with the times, and is stylish and modern. It is obvious that Charlotte is at least a little insane, but in the horror-of-personality films, the supposedly insane exhibit an often remarkable insight. When

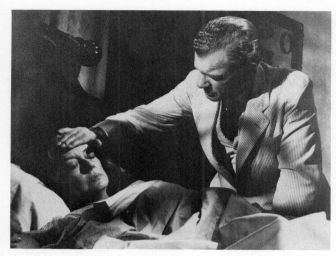

Joseph Cotten and Bette Davis in *Hush, Hush, Sweet Charlotte*

Agnes Moorehead doubts that de Havilland will come, Bette Davis claims assuredly that she'll arrive the next day. And she does. And when de Havilland refuses graciously to help Davis keep the house, Davis accuses her of coming only to try to get her father's money; a fact that, again, turns out to be true. And when Charlotte talks about Jewel Mayhew and claims "she deserves to die," that too turns out to be accurate, for it was Jewel that had killed her husband (and Charlotte's lover) in 1927. Indeed, Aldrich again gives us much information that suggests that Bette Davis is not the treacherous, crazy one. When de Havilland hires some women to help pack, one admits that Charlotte "sure acts crazy sometime; but I wouldn't bet on it." And when Charlotte throws her hate mail on the bed (all from de Havilland), one letter falls to the floor. The maid, Agnes Moorehead, picks it up, and gives it to its sender, Olivia de Havilland: It says "Murderess." The moment is absolutely electrifying in its truthfulness; and, before long, de Havilland *does* murder Moorehead. The film is filled with many striking visual touches. When de Havilland talks about her old romance with Joseph Cotten, the outline of light on the pillar she is leaning against looks exactly like a wedding veil. They acknowledge that the romance had never worked out, and she moves into a more natural, nonsuggestive light. Or later, when she is plotting with Cotten, she very casually turns off the light on Victor Buono's portrait. There are the billowing curtains, the closeup of footsteps, and then the corpse that comes

alive that seem to be direct homages to the film that started it all: *Diabolique*. One of the most interesting visual ideas in *Sweet Charlotte* is Aldrich's photographing Olivia de Havilland through windows. The icon of the window seems a complex one; photographing someone through a window (especially with curtains) suggests that their true nature is inscrutable, hidden, and ultimately evil. I think immediately of the final window image of Bette Davis in William Wyler's *The Little Foxes*, or of the little boy in Richard Mulligan's *The Other*. De Havilland (and never Davis) is photographed three times looking through a window: once when she arrives, a second time after she kills Agnes Moorehead, and a third time before she stages the elaborate masquerade with Joseph Cotten. Ultimately, de Havilland does not survive. When Bette Davis leaves the house triumphantly after discovering the truth and killing her tormentors, she is dressed in modern clothes and leaves her music box, the symbol of her past, behind her. Nevertheless, the attitude of the film can well be represented by a Mary Astor line: "Ruined finery," she says to Cecil

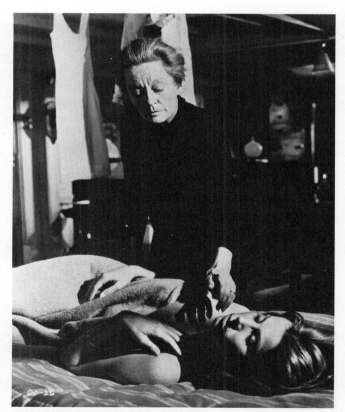

Tallulah Bankhead and Stefanie Powers in *Die, Die, My Darling:* two women in a psychological struggle

31

Kellaway, "that's all I have left." And that is true; for, in this genre, any finery must be ruined. It is not death so much that is horrible, but life. If it is already too late for Bette Davis and Mary Astor and Agnes Moorehead and Olivia de Havilland and for all of us, Mary Astor's poignantly expressed line taken from Alexander Pope, "This long disease, my life," works both as a voluntary metaphor and a reminder of the truly horrible sense of life embodied by this genre.

Especially after *What Ever Happened to Baby Jane?*, Aldrich's first venture into the genre, and certainly after *Hush, Hush, Sweet Charlotte*, his second, the genre became associated very directly with the old movie stars who were increasingly picking them as vehicles for their comebacks. For instance, *Strait-Jacket*, written by *Psycho*'s Robert Bloch and directed by William Castle, gave Joan Crawford the opportunity to be a suspected ax murderess. The film roughly follows the same pattern as the Aldrich films: a crime in the past, the bulk of the story in the present, an emphasis on the relationship between two women (in this case, Diane Baker and Joan Crawford—daughter and mother), and the revelation that madness and guilt is much more complex than it had seemed. *Lady in a Cage*, directed by Walter Grauman in 1964 and starring Olivia de Havilland, was in many ways a departure from the genre. Although de Havilland is presented as a smothering mother who is a lady of leisure, she is never considered either guilty or mad; rather, she undergoes a terrible torture when her house is invaded by an insane young gang led by James Caan and including a rotund Ann Southern. What happens in the film is truly horrible, and no one—not even passing motorists or pedestrians—will stop to help her. *Lady in a Cage* is important for at least two reasons: first, it has a clear and notable visual style unlike the heavy Gothic expressionism of the previous films; and, second, it suggests the direction toward which the genre may be heading—that is, the horror is very specific, unambiguous, and not particularly metaphorical for any more profound general fear. This may be because *Lady in a Cage* is based on a true incident; its horror—a lady's home is invaded senselessly, and no one will help her—can be taken on a purely literal

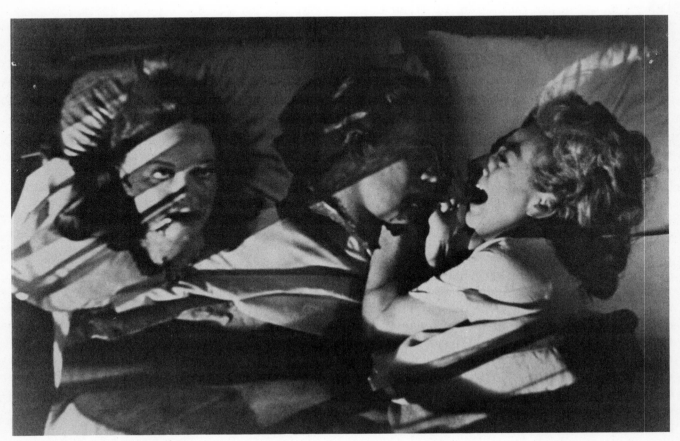

Joan Crawford in *Strait-Jacket*

Lady in a Cage: elevator with no exit as metaphor for an increasingly violent society

Targets was made in 1968 by Peter Bogdanovich and was based on the Charles Whitman killings at the University of Texas. Bogdanovich, a student of film history certainly, uses Boris Karloff as a representative of what the horror film used to be. Within the film, Karloff plays a gentle actor (Byron Orlok) who is a little out of his time. The main thrust of the story, however, is carried by the Bobby Thompson character who (and could there be a more basic American sounding name?) for no reason at all kills his wife, his mother, the delivery boy, and then snipes from atop a gas tank, and then from a drive-in theater, getting confused and stopping only when he is confronted both by Boris Karloff in the flesh and on the screen. The idea of one set of horror values (being embodied by Boris Karloff) confronting another set of horror values (that is, the horror-of-personality values embodied in the Bobby Thompson character) is particularly strong. Although Bobby Thompson is then apprehended, *Targets* can be looked at as a kind of wistful elegy for the kind of supernatural classic horror that is no longer as meaningful as it once was. Most clearly for Bog-

level as a representation of what in the 1960s seemed to be an increasing fear. As such, the film predates *The Boston Strangler, In Cold Blood, 10 Rillington Place, The Incident,* and, most specifically, the genre-oriented *Targets.*

Helpless victim in *Targets:* matricide

33

danovich, the horror of 1968 rests in the mystery and incomprehensibility of Bobby Thompson, who, as he is being taken away says only: "I hardly ever missed, did I?" Bogdanovich does not try to explain Bobby Thompson; he even shuns any psychological conjecture. It was this one reticence that particularly bothered the critics. As Howard Thompson asked obsessively in the *New York Times*:

> Why? This invariable question of today's headlines about the random sniper-murder of innocent people is never answered in *Targets*. This is the only flaw, and a serious one, in this original and brilliant melodrama . . . This one count simply can't be ignored . . . Why? How come?

Once again it seems a critic has missed the obvious point: were an explanation given we could rest easy with the insanity carefully catalogued. It is the very absence of any reason, the very refusal on Bogdanovich's part to give us the slightest grounds for reassurance, that makes *Targets* so disturbing. And it is the germ of *Targets* that can be seen in *Lady in a Cage*.

Another important film during the post-Kennedy assassination period when the genre flourished was *The Nanny*, directed by Seth Holt, and starring Bette Davis. In this film, the question is again one of sanity and of a past crime. Though instead of using two women, Holt uses Bette Davis and a little boy. The climax (with its generic revelation) is simultaneously poignant and repulsive. A similar switch in the formula was made in the 1968 *Pretty Poison*, in which the two protagonists were not two old women, but a young man and a girl in love. Beneath the film's obvious individuality, one can see that *Pretty Poison* really works nicely within the framework of the horror-of-personality film. Anthony Perkins plays the supposedly insane character (and after all, haven't we learned from *Psycho* that the All-American boy is really crazy?), and Tuesday Weld plays the typical, luscious, All-American girl who is a sweet cheerleader with mother problems. Perkins has a crime in his past (having set his house and parents on fire), and has been in an institution. Only after years have passed does Perkins come out of the institution, and the movie begins (like *Baby Jane* or *Sweet Charlotte*, but with the precredit sequences telegraphed into traditional exposition; or like *Strait-Jacket* in particular); yet, as the film goes on, we discover the horrible truth: Perkins, despite being quite decidedly weird, is not the crazy

Bette Davis as *The Nanny* watching Jill Bennett's heart attack

one; rather, it is sweet, nubile Tuesday Weld who is the crazy one. The revelation comes shockingly when Weld very easily kills a guard and then sits on his head in order to drown him. Is this what is happening to American youth? The film is made all the more horrifying because, like *Targets*, the actions of *Pretty Poison* Tuesday Weld are not even explained psychologically—they are merely taken

William Dix in *The Nanny:* Who is insane?

34

Tuesday Weld's All-American Girl and mother Beverly
Garland in *Pretty Poison*

for granted. The irony is that after experiencing the
horror and violence of a supposedly sane person,
Perkins is quite content to go back to the institution,
which he considers safe. And if it's safer to live in
some kind of insane asylum, what does that say for
the basic quality of human nature?

Another important development seems to have
been Curtis Harrington's realization that he could
work in the genre very well. *Games*, made in 1967,
stars Simone Signoret in the same part and in the
only slightly altered plot as *Diabolique*. The power
of the film is basically derived from the density of the
visual images; especially the bizarre set decorations.
Although here, there is no major question of the
ambiguity of insanity, there is the emphasis on the
relationship between two women, and the revelation that one (Signoret, of course) is trying to drive

the other one crazy. There is, however, one
important difference between this film and
Diabolique: In *Diabolique*, Signoret was sincerely
in love with Vera Clouzot's husband. In *Games*,
there is an added twist when Signoret kills James
Caan; and Harrington's vision is revealed as, if not
more sordid, certainly more stylishly bleak than
Clouzot's. Harrington's ideas are continued in *How
Awful About Allan* (a variation in which Anthony
Perkins is pitted against Julie Harris), and particularly in *What's the Matter with Helen?* In this 1970
film, sprightly Debbie Reynolds is pitted against the
mad Shelley Winters. The film is, like *Games*,
remarkably dense in its images: bizarre midgets,
slaughtered rabbits, a little girl impersonating Mae
West, a room full of girls tap-dancing in front of their
rather disgusting mothers, etc. Like Aldrich's *Baby
Jane, What's the Matter with Helen?* is concerned
with Hollywood—and the portrait of Hollywood

35

Catherine Deneuve in *Repulsion:* creeping insanity

Katherine Ross and James Caan in *Games*

that emerges is grotesque and pathetic. For her first straight dramatic role, Harrington lets Debbie Reynolds play a woman who runs away with Winters from the scandal of their children's crime and then starts a dance school that suggests the Mount Hollywood Art School in *Singin' in the Rain*. In fact, the street and exterior of Debbie Reynolds' apartment in *Helen* remarkably echo her street and apartment in *Singin' in the Rain*. It seems that Harrington's intent is to show the underside of that film's Hollywood view; and, indeed, *Helen* does contain at least twenty minutes of singing and dancing. Unlike Aldrich's films, Harrington's do not even have a nominally happy ending; and *Helen* ends with the dead Debbie Reynolds propped up on stage as if to perform, and the dollying camera taking us (although we don't want to go) into a closeup of the now completely deranged Shelley Winters. And it is a horror that not even the attempted relationship with Dennis Weaver can attenuate.

Other later films of the genre include *Twisted Nerve* in 1969, which attempted to explain insanity by equating it with bad chromosomes; *What Ever Happened to Aunt Alice?* in 1969, which pitted old Geraldine Page against the old trooper Ruth Gordon, with the old trooper getting killed; *Who Slew Auntie Roo?* in 1971 with Shelley Winters again as a madwoman; and *Play Misty for Me* in 1971 with Clint Eastwood as the normal one and Jessica Walter as the incomprehensible psychopath who (almost) kills a maid and tries to kill Eastwood. Five of the most recent horror-of-personality films have also been among the most notable: *See No Evil* (1972), starring Mia Farrow as a blind girl terrorized by a

Games: Katherine Ross and Simone Signoret in fatal relationship

Shelley Winters, Debbie Reynolds, and mysterious
stranger in *What's the Matter with Helen?*

What's the Matter with Helen?: two women with secrets of
a monstrous past

Geraldine Page in *What Ever Happened to Aunt Alice?*

The mad Shelley Winters in *Who Slew Auntie Roo?*

Jessica Walter in *Play Misty for Me:* American psychotic

madman; *Frenzy* (1972), a film directed by Alfred Hitchcock about a sex murderer, which was the surprising recipient of near-unanimous raves; *Images* (1972), a film exquisitely photographed by Vilmos Zsigmond and directed by Robert Altman about a young woman's descent into madness; *The Killing Kind* (1974), a reworking of the *Psycho* theme, directed by Curtis Harrington; and *The Legend of Lizzie Borden* (1974), a TV movie directed by Paul Wendkos and starring Elizabeth Montgomery in an amazingly precise and convincing reconstruction of the most famous American murders.

Perhaps the most self-conscious of the horror-of-personality films is Brian De Palma's *Sisters*, made in 1972. Dealing in part with the separation of Siamese twins, *Sisters* represents De Palma's attempt to do homage to Hitchcock by carefully recreating and reinterpreting the many elements of *Psycho*. The film opens with a scene of Lisle Wilson (as Phillip) watching a supposedly blind Margot Kidder (as Danielle) undress, a scene that immediately suggests Hitchcock's fascination with voyeurism. That this scene is ultimately revealed not as reality, but as a set-up television consequence in a clever parody of *Candid Camera* called *Peeping Toms* (with Danielle as an actress playing "jokes" on unsuspecting subjects) suggests the whole fictional and voyeuristic aspect of the cinema itself. From their meeting on the television show, a romance of sorts develops between Phillip and Danielle. While making love with Danielle, Phillip discovers a huge scar on her side, which is later revealed as the result of her separation from her Siamese twin

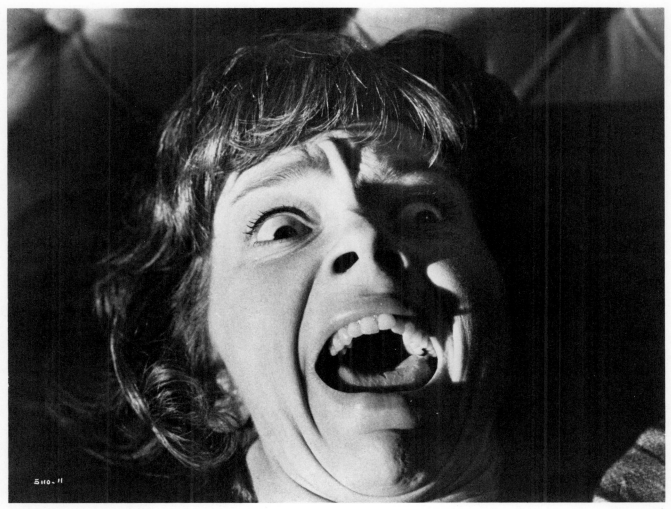

Frenzy: Barbara Leigh-Hunt as victim of rape and strangulation

Dominique. When Phillip returns to Danielle's apartment after buying her a birthday cake, the sleeping form of a woman on the bed suddenly grabs the knife on the cake plate and stabs him repeatedly in the groin and the mouth. Up to this point, Phillip has been treated as the film's protagonist; his sudden murder—apparently by Danielle's psychotic sister, Dominique—strongly resembles the sudden murder of Janet Leigh's Marion in *Psycho*. Indeed, the resemblance is further highlighted by the score's similar orchestration—written, as was the score of *Psycho* twelve years earlier, by Bernard Herrmann. Phillip's death is emotionally harrowing because it is slow and his agony is prolonged; the music shudders and shrieks as Phillip drags himself across the room, leaving a wide trail of blood on the white floor. He does not die until he has managed to write "help" in his own blood on the window—a message that is seen by an investigative reporter, Grace Collier (who is played by Jennifer Salt.) Just as

Sisters: the inevitable generic scene: the disposition of the body

Psycho, in which the murderer does not turn out to be Norman Bates' mother, but Norman Bates himself, in *Sisters*, the murderer does not turn out to be Dominique, but Danielle herself. Danielle is revealed as a split personality who at times takes on the identity of her sister, who, it is revealed, was killed during the operation that separated them. Thus, the *Diabolique*-style relationship between two women (that De Palma borrows from Clouzot) turns out to be the relationship between the two opposite aspects of one split personality. Like Hitchcock, whom he is emulating, De Palma is careful to break up his *mise*-en-*scène* into montage, which takes much advantage of point-of-view shots. De Palma's reworking of *Psycho* is also in part a sexual inversion, with Lisle Wilson's Phillip corresponding to Janet Leigh's Marion; thus, just as

Hitchcock opposes Anthony Perkins' psychotic with the physically similar actor, John Gavin, De Palma opposes Margot Kidder's psychotic with the physically similar actress, Jennifer Salt. Indeed, Jennifer Salt's function in the film as the psychotic's alter ego and unraveller of the mystery parallels the function of *Psycho*'s John Gavin. In this regard, De Palma, like Hitchcock, emphasizes the constant duality of his story, even down to the red designer stripe on the wall of Grace's apartment, paralleling the stripe of blood on the floor of Danielle's apartment. Perhaps the most-striking duality is De Palma's use of split screen: Danielle and her former husband rushing to clean up her apartment and hide Phillip's body on the left image, while Grace and the detective make their way up to Danielle's apartment on the right image. Thus De Palma counterposes the two separate images in the one widescreen frame—a technique that functionally creates suspense and

40

metaphorically suggests the schizophrenic state of Danielle. By the end of the film, the identification between Danielle and her alter ego, Grace, is so complete that in the final hallucinatory flashback, when in the operating room the horrible butcher knife is raised to separate Danielle and Dominique, it is the surrogate image of Grace that we see actually attached to Danielle. When Danielle's schizophrenia is finally unravelled for the audience through Grace's efforts, and when Danielle is taken away by the police, Grace—under hypnotic suggestion from Danielle's former husband—is unable to explain the bizarre events to the baffled police. Instead, a bit crazy now herself, she is compelled to repeat over and over the clearly erroneous statement: "There was no body and there was no murder!" What is madness and what is sanity? As usual, this horror-of-personality film offers no easy answer.

Iconographically, the films of the genre display an amazing consistency. The icons can be divided roughly into three groups: weaponry, locations, and (for lack of a better term) identity symbols. First of all, the weaponry: although the violence in these films is always portrayed with an amazing creativity, the weapons seem to be generally sharp instruments that are not at all exotic. In *Screaming Mimi*, *Psycho*, *Homicidal*, and *What's the Matter with Helen?*, Anita Ekberg, Anthony Perkins, Jean Arless, and Shelley Winters respectively dispatch their victims with a knife. In *Dementia 13*, *Strait-Jacket*, *Twisted Nerve*, *Hush, Hush, Sweet Charlotte*, and, of course, *The Legend of Lizzie Borden*, the weapon is an ax. Other variations include the pointed elevator part in *Lady in a Cage*, the sharp blade of a threshing machine in *What's the Matter with Helen?*, and the saber in *The Mad Room*. The weapon that takes second place is certainly the blunt instrument: the weapon used in *What Ever Happened to Baby Jane?*, *Hush, Hush, Sweet Charlotte*, and others. Other recurring weapons include fire (in *Pyro*, *What Ever Happened to Aunt Alice?*, *Pretty Poison*, and *Who Slew Auntie Roo?*), and, of course, the occasional use of the gun. However, it is interesting to note that the gun is most important in films like *Targets*, which directly and very specifically reflect the fear of unexpected and matter-of-fact violence.

Stella Stevens in *The Mad Room*: Can this vision be evil?

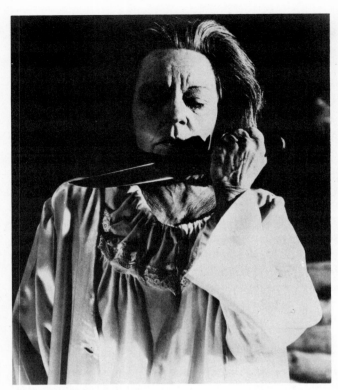

Recurring iconography: the knife in *Die, Die, My Darling*

Recurring iconography: the axe in *Strait-Jacket*

The second group of icons are the locations (and, although I call the third group symbols, it is obvious that the locations in these films often work as metaphors). The most dominant location is, of course, the house. The house is always something frightening, something that is descended from the haunted-house film, but whose terrors are always specifically real rather than mystical. It is the house that contains the dead Mrs. Bates in *Psycho*, the memorabilia in *What Ever Happened to Baby Jane?*, and the suggestion of a once-thriving South in

Hush, Hush, Sweet Charlotte. It is the house in films from *Games* to *The Mad Room* to *Who Slew Auntie Roo?* that reflects the insanity so central to the story. Usually the house is a dead thing, containing memories, corpses, or reminders of an old way of life; the horror usually arises because, while the times change, the house and its occupants do not—such as in *Baby Jane*, *Sweet Charlotte*, *Auntie Roo*, and *Psycho*. There seem to be three particular locations within the house that take on individual importance. First of all, the image in these films of stairways cannot be overemphasized. In *Psycho*, the detective is killed on the stairway. In *Baby Jane*, two of the most important scenes take place there: Joan Crawford trying to get to the telephone, and Bette Davis killing the maid. In *The Psychopath*, the villainess falls down the stairs and is killed. In *The Haunting*, Julie Harris is almost killed by the spiral staircase's jiggling as she tries to discover the mystery of the house and find Richard Johnson's wife. In *Sweet Charlotte*, Agnes Moorehead is killed by Olivia de Havilland and falls down a snakelike staircase; later, as Bette Davis tries to get to her room, she is finally driven crazy as she crawls down the stairway backwards. And in *What's the Matter with Helen?*, the outside rickety stairway works equally as a focal point of the horror. There is a sense in which the stairway works as a gateway between two separate domains. In *Baby Jane*, it takes us from the crazy domain of Bette Davis to what seems the more reasonable domain of Joan Crawford. In *What's the Matter with Helen?* it works the same way. In fact, there is a particularly horrifying scene in *Helen* in which the sane Debbie Reynolds comes down the stairway into the mad Shelley Winters' domain and discovers the butchered rabbits. In this film, the stairway separates the two domains: mad from sane. In some of the other films, especially *Sweet Charlotte*, the use of the stairway is more complicated; for instance, although it would seem that the mad domain would be the upstairs room of Bette Davis, all the crazy goings-on take place on the first floor: the supposedly sane domain. The end of *Sweet Charlotte*, with the revelation that de Havilland is really a villainess and that Charlotte is, for all her problems, remarkably sane, makes it clear why the "mad portion" of the film never took place in Bette Davis' upstairs domain, but rather in de Havilland's—with the climaxes taking place on the stairway. Although complicated, the stairway remains a tenuous gateway, a gateway that when crossed over is always terrifying and, for someone, usually fatal. The two other locations in the house that are particularly important are the bathroom and the basement. The bathroom's importance is easy to understand: it is the room of the house that is the most personal, the room that is used to cleanse the body, to make it pure. Hence, whenever violence takes place in this room, it is particularly obscene and upsetting. There is the bathtub scene in *Diabolique*; the famous shower murder in *Psycho*; the orgy in *Lady in a Cage*; the image of a vulnerable Glynis Johns in a bathtub in the 1962 remake of *The Cabinet of Caligari*; Samantha Eggar being tied in the bathtub in *The Collector*; and the horrible "drowning in a bathtub" scene in *The Nanny*. The recurring cellar image is probably related to the womb and/or darkness. Thus we have the irony of Anthony Perkins putting his mother in the womb of the house in *Psycho*, or of Tallulah Bankhead in her little underground dungeon in *Die, Die, My Darling*. Perhaps the best example, one that clearly unites the idea of the cellar with perverted sexuality, is that of *The Collector*, in which Terence Stamp

Tuesday Weld on stairway in *Pretty Poison* after killing her mother—but Tuesday was supposed to be sane. . . .

The archetypal location of the genre: Anthony Perkins recoiling from the blood-soaked bathroom in *Psycho*

The stairway as metaphor for the line between sanity and madness: Julie Harris and Anthony Perkins in *How Awful About Allan*

Identity synbols: Janet Leigh and reflection in *Psycho*—is she insane or is she normal?

Hywel Bennett and reflection in *Twisted Nerve*

kidnaps Samantha Eggar and deposits her in a little underground apartment. Aside from the house, the other main location that continually appears is the mental institution—a location whose literalness needs no explanation. Institutions appear in *Maniac*, *Straight-Jacket*, *The Nanny*, *Shock Treatment*, *Screaming Mimi*, *The Cabinet of Caligari*, *Nightmare*, and *Pretty Poison*.

The last group of icons that appears with regularity are the identity symbols. These are all objects that reflect on the characters' identity and (in)sanity. For instance, there are the dolls and/or puppets that are in *Baby Jane, Bunny Lake is Missing*, and *The Psychopath*. There are the photographs and paintings in *Baby Jane, Sweet Charlotte, Die, Die, My Darling, Repulsion*, and *What's the Matter with Helen?*; the mirrors in *Sweet Charlotte*, and *Repulsion*; the movie screen and the camera in *Baby Jane, Sweet Charlotte, What's the Matter with Helen?*, and *Peeping Tom*; the recurring windows in all the films; the statues in *Screaming Mimi* and *Games*; and

Joan Crawford (left) must come to terms with her past
(right) in *Strait-Jacket:* Is she a murderess?

The juxtaposition of supposedly sweet Olivia de Havilland
with a bird of prey in *Hush, Hush, Sweet Charlotte*

the birds in *Psycho*, the parakeet and rat in *Baby Jane*, and the rabbits in *Helen*. The question of identity and sanity is presented especially succinctly in *Sweet Charlotte*. When Charlotte opens the door in the dark and the photographer rudely takes her

Iconic symbology in *The Psychopath*

The Psychopath: crazed proliferation of identity symbols

picture, she recoils, not only because of the shock, but because of the realization of what her identity really is. At the end of the film a photographer again asks for her picture; but this time she smiles, quite able to accept her identity now that her sanity is almost intact and the guilt is off her shoulders. In *Baby Jane*, the crushed doll head works as a marvelous symbol for Bette Davis' sanity. And, in the same film, the scream that Bette Davis gives out after seeing herself in the mirror is truly heart-rending. The discrepancy between self-concept and image, or ideal and reality, is further illustrated by the shot in *Baby Jane* when the painting of a young Joan Crawford is juxtaposed over the Joan Crawford that looks like a corpse. Can there be any other group of movies in which identity symbols recur so consistently? Again, the concern with identity and sanity nicely mirrors the often-heard sixties' question: "Who am I?" It is this genre's answer to this question that is particularly disturbing.

Ironically, just as the various concerns of the fifties and sixties seemed to end the classic horror film, the spreading concern with what seems to be a

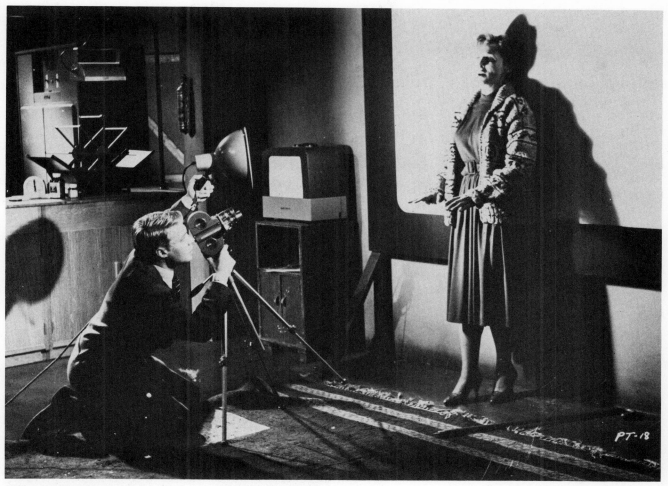

Carl Boehm and Moira Shearer in *Peeping Tom:* the camera, lights, and movie screen representing Boehm's voyeuristic obsession—and, by implication, the obsession of the filmgoer

fear of the possible innate insanity and violence in man seems to be headed perhaps toward eradicating the clear distinctions between the horror-of-personality films like *Targets* and what would seem to be nonhorror films like *The Boston Strangler, 10 Rillington Place, In Cold Blood, Deliverance, The Wild Bunch, Straw Dogs, A Clockwork Orange,* and *Dirty Harry.* Horror films have always reflected man's deepest anxieties about himself. In a time where life, or at least man's awareness of it, seems to be increasingly horrible, it is most understandable that elements from the horror-of-personality films

(violence, insanity) are now being fed into the mainstream. No longer are horror films (if they ever really were) escapist fare for children. Hopefully, critics will realize that the "strict" horror-of-personality films—films such as *Psycho, What Ever Happened to Baby Jane?, Hush, Hush, Sweet Charlotte, Play Misty for Me,* and *What's the Matter with Helen?,* films that have been previously dismissed or ridiculed as shocking, gory, silly, excessive, and violent—can, through considerations of genre, show as much about our society and be as artistic a statement on man's concerns and his nature as films like *Straw Dogs* and *A Clockwork Orange*—works that largely because of their *auteur* considerations have already been accepted as worthy of study.

47

"Watch the skies . . ."—from *The Thing*

"Mitch, this isn't normal, is it?"—Tippi Hedren in *The Birds*

"I will not capitulate!"—Bérenger's last words in *Rhinoceros*

"Lady, it's the end of the world . . ."—Bum in *The Birds*

2

THE HORROR OF ARMAGEDDON

If the horror-of-personality films are both a clear reflection of the fears of the sixties and yet a departure from the linear development of the horror film in the fifties, the second new subgenre of horror film, which I call the horror of Armageddon, continues the linear development of the horror film from the science-fiction horror of the fifties into a more pure horror film, which deals, nevertheless, with most of the same issues and ideas as its precursors. The archetypal horror-of-Armageddon film is Alfred Hitchcock's *The Birds;* in this subgenre, the world is constantly being threatened with extinction, usually by nonhuman, unindividualized creatures such as birds, bats, bees, frogs, snakes, rabbits, ants, or plants. Although the nucleus of the horror-of-Armageddon subgenre is distinct, the outer reaches of the subgenre are downright fuzzy; indeed, the horror of Armageddon includes in its periphery films as disparate as *Yog, Monster from Outer Space* (Japan, 1970), *The War Game* (Britain, 1965), and *They Shoot Horses, Don't They?* (USA, 1969). Before going into a detailed discussion of the horror-of-Armageddon films, it is first important to understand exactly what these films drew upon and from where they descended.

The monsters of the thirties and forties horror film gave way in the fifties to a horror that was almost united with science fiction. Perhaps the two archetypal horror films of the fifties are *The Thing,* directed by Christian Nyby in 1951 (with some of the direction often credited to Howard Hawks), and *Five,* directed by Arch Oboler in the same year. Each film dealt specifically with a major horror science-fiction theme: *The Thing* with the idea that

there exists some life on other planets that could threaten life on earth; and *Five* with the idea that the earth could be destroyed virtually by the atomic bomb and subsequent radiation. Thus, both horror films dealt with the unearthly: *The Thing* with its creature from outer space, and *Five* with its re-creation of an earth stripped of all those things, such as flora, fauna, and civilization, which normally make up the operative iconography of "earthliness." In *The Thing,* the outer-space creature was something to be feared; that is, a monster in the best horror tradition. Note how in *The Day the Earth Stood Still,* directed by Robert Wise in the same year, the civilized amiability of the superiority of Michael Rennie's outer-space creature turns that film into strict unhorrific science fiction. Like so many of the fifties horror films, *The Thing* ended with the admonition that we should watch the skies; and, although I'm sure Christian Nyby didn't mean for us to watch the skies for birds, when *The Birds* came in 1962, the emotional effect was similar. In a malevolent universe, one is not allowed to be complacent; one of the strongest images in *The Birds,* largely derived from *The Thing* fear in the fifties films, is that of the little girls looking tearfully up to the skies after the birds have mysteriously attacked them and then disappeared. *The Thing,* like *The Birds,* and rats, and rabbits to come, is something mysterious and inexplicable. *The Thing* does not violate our civilization's rules of conduct or the universe's natural order; it merely conducts itself completely independent of these things—and therein lies the horror.

The mythic patterns of *Five* are by now very

49

Five: a post-Armageddon Eden with Susan Douglas as Woman

familiar to us: with the world destroyed by the atomic bomb and its radiation, it is now up to a nucleus of individuals to somehow continue the civilization even if, (and this is the overfamiliar part) there is only one truly desirable female; which, of course, the fifties morality would not allow the men to share. The one desirable female is often the daughter of the scientist figure, who, in the aftermath of the atomic fallout, is often rightly and skeptically viewed as a defeated, rumpled figure whose authority is gradually eroded by the villain's quest for power. The villain's secondary quest is generally the seduction of the "innocent," desirable female. The hero figure is usually young, attractive, thoughtful, very physical, and eager to protect the heroine. The archetypal atomic-survival film often ends with only the hero and heroine alive: as Adam and Eve figures ejected from the Garden of Civilization and having to cope not with the guilt of the Original Sin, but with the guilt of the Ultimate Sin: the destruction of all life on the earth; their only expiation is in trying to repopulate and renew the civilization on their own. Note that, in an important sense, the horror science-fiction movie is very close to the Frankenstein story with the atomic bomb representing the monster. Are there some things into which man must not delve? In *Five* and the other atomic-survival films, the atomic Frankenstein has created its havoc, destroying itself, often its creators, and all civilization. The mad scientist is shown to be, in a quite complex sense, sociologically and humanistically mad. But now that there is nothing left, what next? These movies start where

the Frankenstein movies leave off. And even survival in this postatomic nether world is no easy task because the survivors' safe little area is often surrounded by hostile mutants anxious to attack and kill for no reason other than the fact that their existential purpose in the film is to attack and kill. Thus in this pattern of nonhuman, unindividualized creatures attacking, we already have a major element of the horror of Armageddon.

The word "Armageddon" comes, of course, from the Bible, and is the name of the place where the last battle between the forces of good and evil is supposed to take place. I use the term not because of its connotations of good and evil (for in this genre what is good is often intermingled with what is evil), but because these films always deal with a struggle that is obviously ultimate, mythical, and soul-rending. The final bird attack in *The Birds* transcends itself; these birds are not merely birds, they are a metaphor for existential struggle and horror. If every bird in the last frame of that film were to disappear, the horror would remain; it is the knowledge that the birds are "out there" that is horrifying. The term Armageddon also seems relevent because there seems to be a strong relationship between these films and many of the stories in the Bible; for instance, the many plagues sent out to express the wrath of God, or even more dramatically the most archetypal story in the Bible: the flood. Take God away from the flood, and you have a true horror-of-Armageddon movie: Suddenly, out of the sky, it begins to rain. What was previously considered a normal aspect of nature turns abnormal when the rain starts acting unlike rain and refuses to stop. The rain attacks and kills everyone; only Noah and his family manage to survive the existential test by working hard to hold tightly onto their floating house. Ultimately, a rainbow appears as congratulations and in promise that the existential horror has come to an end. The pattern is exactly that of *The Birds*, only Hitchcock refuses us the satisfaction of the horror-releasing rainbow. The use of the word Armageddon also has a modern relevence: while ancient peoples could easily imagine an Armageddon caused by God, modern man can all too easily imagine an Armageddon caused, not by God, but by man. Armageddon is the "war to end all wars," the ultimate confrontation; in short, the atomic bomb. If Hiroshima and Nagasaki marked the beginning of Armageddon, then *On the Beach* and *Dr.*

Another post-Armageddon society in *The Time Machine:*
Can our violent destiny be prevented?

Media report on the arrival of the flying saucer in *The Day
the Earth Stood Still*

Strangelove marked the fictional Armageddon's final paroxysm.

The three great themes of the horror of Armageddon are

1) proliferation,
2) besiegement, and
3) death.

What makes the formal enumeration of these themes interesting is that they are precisely the same great themes of the French-Rumanian playwright, Eugène Ionesco. Ionesco's "theatre of the absurd" has been widely acclaimed; the obvious similarity between Ionesco's *oeuvre* and the horror of Armageddon is testament, I think, to the relevance of both. Accepted by the intellectuals, Ionesco's plays, although they spring from an individual man with a specific background, deal nevertheless with the same fears and concerns that seem to spring unconsciously from the mass of minds of the thousands of men who have worked on the horror of Armageddon. If Ionesco is an individual genius, it

Explosion in *The Thing:* Is this the way the world ends, not with a whimper, but a bang?

the new tenant giving the men directions and arranging the furniture according to his predetermined plan. Gradually the men begin moving in the furniture faster and faster until there is no space left in the room. The new tenant insists that all the furniture will fit, for he claims that he has carefully measured the room. Suddenly, the furniture starts moving in by itself without the aid of the movers; in short, behaving quite unlike furniture usually behaves! Furniture comes in from both sides, from the ceiling, through the windows. We hear reports that the furniture is causing traffic jams outside as well; indeed, it has damned up the Seine River, besieging Paris as well as the little room. The play ends as the stage is completely filled, and the new tenant is literally buried in the furniture. As the moving men leave, the new tenant very calmly asks them to turn off the light.

The similarity between *The New Tenant* and *The Birds* is obvious. Structurally they are the same: starting from banality, moving gradually to the extraordinary, and inexorably to the horrific. In both works the emphasis is on the besiegement of one area (the room, the house across Bodega Bay), although we hear reports that other areas are under similar attack. In both, the inexplicability of the proliferation creates the horror. The main difference between the two works, of course, is in that which is chosen as the metaphorical symbol of the existential forces (although, it must be pointed out, both birds and furniture, which are generally considered homely and benign, are bizarre and original choices for monster-horror figures). Perhaps the most interesting thing about the horror of Armageddon is in the way the choice of the metaphorical proliferated horror sharply affects the overall meaning and thrust of the work. "The world is too much with us," the furniture in *The New Tenant* seems to be saying; there is no escaping from civilization—wherever you go, it will follow you out to torment and horrify you.

Ionesco's next horror-of-Armageddon, theatre-of-the absurd play—and the one for which he is primarily known—is, of course, *Rhinoceros*. Again, *Rhinoceros* starts with a scene of banality: the Everyman figure Bérenger (the recurring character in Ionesco's work) is sitting outside a French café talking to a friend, while at the next table a logician babbles on endlessly, fracturing logic. Suddenly, a rhinoceros charges past them. There is some argument as to whether the rhinoceros had one horn or

may be because he consciously was able to work out these themes years before they emerged as mass-media, popular-culture concerns. Ionesco:

> To discover the fundamental problem common to all mankind, I must ask myself what *my* fundamental problem is, what *my* ineradicable fear is. I am certain then to find the problems and fears of literally everyone. That is the true road into my own darkness, our darkness, which I try to bring to the light of day.[1]

Ionesco's three plays that most clearly correspond to the horror of Armageddon are *The New Tenant (Le Nouveau Locataire)* written in 1953, *Rhinoceros* in 1958, and *The Killing Game (Jeux de Massacre)* in 1970; the latter of which bears an astounding resemblance to that horror-of-Armageddon masterpiece *Night of the Living Dead.*

His one-act play *The New Tenant* may be Ionesco's most successfully realized creation. It opens typically both for Ionesco and for the genre with a scene of overriding banality. A talkative *concierge* is preparing an absolutely empty room for her new tenant; she quite busily talks out the window, expending all sorts of energy while doing absolutely nothing. When the new tenant finally arrives, he is a dapper, quiet, thoughtful, introspective, Everyman. He tells the *concierge* he will take the room, but refuses her help. As she leaves a bit irritated, the moving men start moving in the tenant's furniture; and it is the moving of the furniture that makes up the bulk of the play. At first, it comes in quite nicely,

[1]Eugène Ionesco, "The Playwright's Role," *London Observer,* June 29, 1958.

Dana Wynter and Kevin McCarthy flee the conformity of the mob in *Invasion of the Body Snatchers:* "I will not capitulate!"

two, and discussion as to where it came from. Before long it becomes clear that rather than fight the stampeding rhinoceroses, everyone is instead gradually turned into rhinoceroses. As "rhinoceritis" reaches its frenzied peak, and Bérenger sees first his best friend turn into a rhinoceros before his eyes and then even witnesses his girl friend's defection (compare *Rhinoceros* with Don Siegel's *Invasion of the Body Snatchers* of the same period, especially the Kevin McCarthy-Bérenger and Dana Wynter-Daisy parallels), Bérenger decides, albeit reluctantly, that *"Je ne capitule pas!"* ("I will not capitulate!"). Again the structural and thematic relationship between *Rhinoceros* and the horror of Armageddon is clear. What is most interesting about *Rhinoceros* is its metaphorical aspects. Rhinoceroses, unlike birds and furniture, are already slightly frightening. Although much has

been written suggesting that the rhinoceroses are a simple metaphor for Nazis, this is really a simplistic solution—a solution that was so widely accepted when the play first came out that the play *Rhinoceros* is now being widely rejected as overrated and simplistic itself (the 1973 film version Americanized the play into an anti-Nixon liberal tract). The critics should instead discard their initial simplistic evaluation. The play is not merely anti-Nazi, but anti-Communist as well; the symbol of the rhinoceros works as an image of any totalitarian state where free speech, human dignity, and individualism are prohibited. As such, rather than being a political and Brechtian *pièce à thèse*, *Rhinoceros* is a profoundly antipolitical and prohumanistic work. Its emphasis is not on the evil of all politics as much as on the influence of this evil on our Everyman: Bérenger. At the end of the play the rhinoceroses have Bérenger in an almost schizophrenic state of longing to be beautifully green with horns, yet adamant about retaining his identity as an individu-

Invasion of the Body Snatchers: last-chance warning

al. The rhinoceroses are truly living dead, for they have no identity; that last act of *Rhinoceros,* in which Bérenger watches helplessly as all his values—friendship, loyalty, and romantic love—are stripped away as everyone turns into dreaded rhinoceroses, is truly his *Night of the Living Dead,* and a night as dark as that in any horror film. The image of the rhinoceros herd is a faceless unindividualized one; the mass of rhinoceroses instantly relates to the columns of faceless Nazis united behind Hitler, or, even more strongly, the masses of Chinese in Maoist China, united in their work suits, faceless in their sameness. There is something about this robotized sameness that relates to the mathematical precision of atomic technology. The end of this century's cataclysmic fifth decade marked 1) the defeat of

Invasion of the Body Snatchers: not rhinoceroses, but peapods

Hitler and his masses; 2) the revolution of Mao and his masses; and 3) the scientific breakthrough in the atomic bombing of the masses at Hiroshima and Nagasaki. There is even a link between this unindividualized proliferation of totalitarian masses in the forties with the proliferation of a population explosion and eventual ecological concerns in the sixties. Indeed, the remarkable capacity of the proliferated symbol to work as a metaphor for so many different kinds of concerns, which all relate nevertheless to the end of World War II, is one of the hallmarks of the horror of Armageddon.

While Ionesco created *The New Tenant* in 1953 and *Rhinoceros* in 1958, it took the movies a little longer before coming up with much the same formulas. Perhaps the first horror film that comes close to the horror of Armageddon is *Them* in 1954 with James Arness. A little girl is found almost out of her mind on the highway, muttering over and over the one word: "Them . . ." Gradually, we discover that "them" refers to giant ant mutations that proceed to wreak havoc in Los Angeles. *Them* is really a transitional film; largely science fiction, it uses the idea of atomic mutation to explain away the giant ants. Furthermore, the use of giant ants, rather than normal-sized ants, suggests a slightly more specifically fantastic (and thus less existential) kind of horror. Nevertheless, the giant ants clearly relate more to *The Birds* than to the traditional King Kong type of monster. While King Kong, the animal monsters in *Dinosaurus!*, and even the giant spider in *The Lost World*, clearly represent man's animalistic nature and his past, the ants in *Them* are the beginning of a new tradition because they represent the most complex scientific leanings of man and his future. The irony is that, after millions of years of development, man's scientific necessity to investigate areas into which man should not delve is bringing him back to the same point of horror from which he had been working those millions of years to escape. Out of the frying pan of King Kong we go into the fire of mutant grasshoppers, unable to hold onto that tentative balance between inhuman savagery and inhuman overcivilization.

The Beginning of the End, 1957, featuring James Arness' brother Peter Graves, covered much the same ground as *Them,* only this time the metaphorical object of proliferation was gigantic grasshoppers. An extremely low-budget film entitled *The Killer Shrews* followed in 1959; and, while *The Killer Shrews* comes close to being one of those laughable

Them: atomic mutation

Them: the proliferation of unindividualized creatures

horror films, it is most interesting to study neverthe-less. In this film, we again get the archetypal fifties pattern of characters: there is the logical scientist, the desirable girl, the coward who wants power, and the hero. The scientist has been experimenting with the genetic acceleration of little rats; to his amaze-ment and ultimate stupefaction, what resulted was not superintelligent rats, but horrible killer shrews. The low-budget special effects are ludicrously in-ferior to the effects of later films like *The Birds*; the shrews appear to be rather docile dogs covered with tar and straw, with an occasional insert of a stuffed, fanged head edited in for good measure. Neverthe-less, these creatures take on a rather adult, existen-tial meaning. Almost the entire film takes place inside the house of the scientist as it is constantly besieged at night by the killer shrews. And this is only right, for it is in the night that we are the most susceptible to our fears. There are some very powerful scenes of people running crazily to get back in the house while the fanged shrews frenziedly chase them. Some of the scenes work powerfully despite their amateurish execution because they tie into a kind of universal childhood fear: the recurring dream of so many children of being chased by a vicious and gigantic dog. Invariably in these dreams, your feet are like lead, the house door is locked, you fumble with the key, you trip over the stoop, etc. For some reason some of the very "worst" and most amateurish horror films constantly surprise us by tying into these fears so effortlessly. *The Killer Shrews* also contains one of the classical archetypal moments: the superlogical scientist who very calmly records his own responses up to his own death, so as to leave an official, properly scientific record. The unlikely climax of *The Killer Shrews* takes place when, after a final horrible night of besiegement by the shrews, the hero, the heroine, and her father make their escape from the house by duckwalking in upside-down cans to the beach, where they are able to survive the night by immersing themselves in the water, which luckily stops the shrews who do not swim. Even in such a crude film, the water works symbolically as a kind of river of life that simultane-ously rebaptizes the characters in a more natural faith, and repudiates the modern faithless science that created the shrews.

And next comes the seminal film of the genre: Alfred Hitchcock's *The Birds*. Like Ionesco's plays, *The Birds* starts with a scene of banality: Tippi Hedren (playing Melanie Daniels) trying to play a

Rod Taylor in *The Birds*: birds in cages

rather pointless joke on Rod Taylor (playing Mitch Brenner) by pretending to be an employee at a bird store. People who see the film only once remember in retrospect only the bird attacks; in actuality, most of the film is a rather clever comedy of manners, the bird attacks providing the *frissons* and the focus, but certainly not the film's nucleus. Just as the rhinoceroses in *Rhinoceros* may tend to obscure the fact that the play is about the character of Bérenger, the birds obscure the fact that *The Birds* is about the relationships between the three main characters and the importance of those relationships in human terms. Even the bird attacks are in some bizarre way comic; there are terrifying yet absurd images of an outdoor children's party in which the children run from . . . birds, an old woman suddenly hysterical because her farmhouse is being filled with . . . sparrows, the birds watching while a group of people are being kept virtually caged in a roadside inn. The relationship between comedy and horror in Hitch-cock's films, as well as in Ionesco's plays, is often that of synthesis. (One thinks as far back as Hitchcock's *Sabotage*, where a soon-to-be-committed stabbing is juxtaposed with the animated cartoon "Who Killed Cock Robin?") There is something about Hitchcock's and Ionesco's type of comedy that is, if not more tragic than tragedy, certainly more pes-simistic; for, if classical tragedy deals overtly with the problems and pains of existence, comedy, although dealing with the same problems, tends to disguise these thematic and essentially disturbing concerns by emphasizing instead its invitation to laughter or amusement. Hitchcock may have re-

Children's party in *The Birds*

garded *The Birds* as one elaborate joke constructed from the comic premise of reversing the traditional relationship between bird and man, but the joke is a dark one: can there be human dignity when a society woman, a farmer, and even innocent children can be attacked by birds at any moment? J.L. Styan's description of Ionesco's style works very well to describe Hitchcock's own style in *The Birds*:

> He has a talent for presenting his characters . . . as immobile puppets in a world that is alive and constantly threatening . . . It is knock-about charade . . . where Grand Guignol violence surrounds the unconscious victims, and the walls rock ironically round their doomed heads. . . . It is the method of classical comedy grown cruel and cold, and its satire grown hysterical.[2]

[2]J. L. Styan, *The Dark Comedy* (Cambridge, England, Cambridge University Press, 1962), p. 232.

Although *The Birds* is visually a very bright film with all the horror taking place in broad daylight, it is as thematically dark as *Psycho*, its possibly fruitless suggestion to "only connect" in order to make this malevolent universe bearable, disguised under layers of special-effects set pieces. There has been much discussion as to what, if anything, the attacks of the birds are supposed to represent; excellent and persuasive analysis has been provided by Robin Wood in his book *Hitchcock's Films*. Certainly Hitchcock has gone a step beyond *Them* and *The Killer Shrews*; the birds are not explained away through the device of a scientist whose genetic injections simply went out of control. The key to the puzzle lies in the café scene (compare with the café scene in *Rhinoceros* which serves the same purpose) in which Hitchcock has various characters volunteer their own explanations. The birds are a punishment

The Birds: "A world that is alive and constantly threatening"

Rod Taylor and Tippi Hedren in The Birds: "Only connect"

from God; they mean the end of the world; they mean that nature is getting even; they come to criticize the attitudes of Melanie Daniels—all these are suggested only to be rejected. Descended from the atomic-bomb age of anxiety, *The Birds* no longer represents the atomic bomb, but simply that existential anxiety; the birds themselves are the horror—the sickness, the death, the violence, the cruelty, the absurdity—any horror that is at any moment capable of coming seemingly from nowhere, and which, whether created by man or sent without explanation, is quite simply part of the very nature of things. In short, *The Birds* works as a metaphor for the human condition. The brilliant ambiguous ending allows the viewer, through the substitution of his own view of life, to decide what will happen (just as in the climax of *Rhinoceros*). Completely surrounded by birds, will Mitch's family and Melanie escape this death, or will they discover more birds at the end of the road which will peck them to pieces even more ferociously? When one considers that most horror films end happily (that is, Frankenstein and Dracula are, albeit temporarily, destroyed, or the giant grasshoppers are repelled), *The Birds*, along with *Psycho*, is one of the few horror films up to this time to which the question—"Does it have a happy ending?"—is unanswerable. Indeed, the final moment of *The Birds* is at the same time its most suspenseful and yet the moment that most clearly approaches total stasis. In the final moment the birds do not move (just as in *Psycho*'s final moment, Anthony Perkins refuses to "even bat that fly"). It is this stasis that is so horrifyingly bleak. One again thinks of Ionesco's plays: the final scene in *The New Tenant* when the gentleman is completely buried in furniture and cannot move; the ambiguity of Bérenger's final "*Je ne capitule pas!*" in *Rhinoceros* when we do not truly know if he is going to survive as a human being; the final horrible tableau in *The Chairs (Les Chaises)* when the stage is completely covered with chairs and invisible people; or the last act of *The Killer (Tueur sans Gages)* in which after two acts of madcap

The Birds: "My God . . . what can we do . . . what can we do. . . ."

movement the Everyman, Bérenger, finds the Killer and delivers a fifteen-page monologue on why the Killer should not kill, only to have the Killer chuckle, raise his knife, and take a step closer to Bérenger who lowers his head and asks, "My God . . . what can we do . . . what can we do . . ." as the curtain swiftly descends before the audience can see the ultimate outcome. In *The Birds*, we can try to love one another and to establish relationships, but whether this will accomplish anything is unclear. Though "the bridge is love, the only survival, and the only meaning," will that bridge nevertheless break and precipitate its travellers into the gulf below?

If there is a gulf below, exactly what is it that is above? In *The Birds*, the object of proliferation is only slightly more important than the object of besiegement; that is, the farmhouse. In *The Killer Shrews*, the house that was besieged was strangely devoid of any meaning: at one point a character tried ineffectually to escape the shrews by going into the cellar (the womb), but the house had no distinctive definition apart from "the world of science." In *The Birds*, the house is much more important. The first inclination of the characters is not to escape from the house, but to cling to it; the home is quite clearly a place of comfort and safety. The school is not safe (for it has big windows), the town of Bodega Bay and, hence, civilization is not safe (for the birds absolutely control it), Suzanne Pleshette is killed when she goes outside the house, and the little girl is saved because Suzanne Pleshette struggled to push her inside the house to safety. Although Dan Fawcett is attacked and killed in his house, he is attacked while asleep, and there is the clear sense of the house being raped. In the horror-of-personality films, the house was inevitably a dark, dead place of memories, a place of corruption, secrets, and unhealthy twists. The house in much of the horror of Armageddon, when it appears, works differently: it is a symbol of family life, a symbol of the materialism that allows us to organize our lives (Jessica Tandy very patiently fooling with her coffee cups), even a symbol (with Tippi Hedren's piano playing and the house's furnishings) of self-expression, of folk culture. The house is never so safe as when the fireplace is lit, prohibiting the birds from attacking down the chimney, yet creating a mythic Hestia-warmth within. Although as a symbol the house is something to hold onto, it is eventually only a symbol: it must be given up when the birds threaten to destroy it.

Rod Taylor and Jessica Tandy in *The Birds:* the house as a symbol of the materialism that allows us to organize our lives

Family culture and family must inevitably be carried out and continued, not by the house, but by the characters who truly feel for each other and can carry those feelings with them wherever they go, building on the past only as a foundation for some hopefully to be fulfilled future.

The next horror-of-Armageddon film is *The Day of the Triffids,* an ingenious little film based on the novel by John Wyndham. In this film, a meteor shower causes the proliferation of triffids; which are voracious, self-locomoted, man-eating plants. Ultimately there is a happy ending as the triffids are killed by seawater. (The pattern here harkens back to *War of the Worlds,* where the Martians are killed, not by the men who are fighting them, but by the "natural" bacteria of the earth.) Yet even in *The Day*

of the Triffids, the big scene is when an army of triffids besieges a farmlike house. Other films in this series include *The Deadly Bees* in 1967, which used bees as the object of proliferation, and *Eye of the Cat* in 1969, which used cats. In addition to starring Eleanor Parker in her second wheelchair, *Eye of the Cat* featured the deservedly classic though certainly erroneous observation that "French directors have gone from Marienbad to worse."

Meanwhile, in 1970, Jacques Demy was working on a musical remake of that rat extravaganza, *The Pied Piper,* starring Donovan as the piper. Demy was sending his rushes back to the Hollywood studio, but the executives kept sending them back to him with the comment: "Yes, very nice, but do you have to show all those rats? They're really quite nasty, distasteful, little things. Perhaps you can leave them out of the story somehow." Demy reportedly was still continuing his work, putting

Carol Ann Ford tries to escape the siege of the plants in
The Day of the Triffids

The Day of the Triffids: mass panic

Janette Scott being attacked by plants in *The Day of the
Triffids*

Donovan as *The Pied Piper*

aside the constant memos to cut down on the rats, when he suddenly started getting memos saying: "More rats. We like the rats. Give us more closeups of the rats."

The sudden turnabout of the sponsoring studio was of course the result of the film that proved rats were big box-office, the film that reactivated the genre with a vengeance: *Willard*. An all-time moneymaker, *Willard* is the story of a friendless young man who makes friends with a pack of rats. When Willard's mother dies and the villain of the piece, played by Ernest Borgnine, threatens to foreclose on the mortgage, Willard sends his rats into action: they kill Borgnine. Interestingly, the house in *Willard* is used more like the house in *Psycho*—as a kind of sick depository, a tomb to the past. Although it is clear that Ernest Borgnine's motives in wanting the house are entirely self-serving, it is just as clear that Willard alone cannot manage the house on his finances, and would be truly better off both financially and mentally were he to get rid of the house. But Willard is unlike the typical horror-of-Armageddon protagonist; like Anthony Perkins in *Psycho*, he is mentally disturbed. After the death of Borgnine, Willard tries to make some sort of human contact with the beautiful

heroine, played by Sondra Locke, but the rats get in the way. Making her leave the house, Willard realizes that he has created a monster and must get rid of his rats. At this point the irony becomes clear: Willard is no longer master of his rats; rather, Ben, the biggest rat, has somehow managed to acquire both a superior intelligence and complete control of the other rats. Before Willard is able to complete his extermination plan, the rats attack and kill him, while their leader Ben watches. The ending is really surprisingly bleak, allowing Ben and the rats to survive so they can appear in their own sequel *Ben*, the following year. The fear of rats, notoriously the scavengers and garbage pickers of the animal world, seems to be almost universal. If *Willard* and *Ben* do not seem to be the overwhelmingly disturbing works that *The Birds* and *The New Tenant* seem to be, it may be because we are more delighted and aesthetically moved by the awesome and ironic creation of a horrific world composed of traditionally harmless birds or furniture than by the less-awesome creation of a horrific world composed of traditionally frightening rats.

As the box office went wild over rats, the genre flourished. The next notable film in the genre was *Night of the Lepus*, in which huge rabbits ravage a countryside. *Night of the Lepus* tried to take advantage of many of the same elements as *The Birds*, in that the rabbit is essentially a loveable creature; although the *Lepus* creators made the rabbits fifteen feet tall (and the mouth of a gigantic rabbit is peculiarly unnerving). Just as in *The Birds*, where birds in cages are ironically juxtaposed later

Sondra Locke in *Willard*: the generic idea that love has a slight chance to prevent catastrophic personal destiny

62

Bruce Davison with Socrates and Ben in *Willard*

Horror in *Ben*

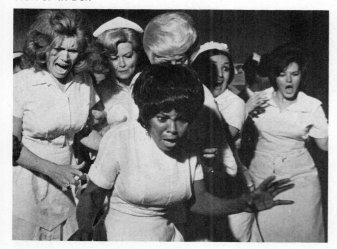

with birds attacking men in cages, *Night of the Lepus* opens with documentary scenes of men killing rabbits, then builds gradually to a climax where giant rabbits kill men. If there is throughout the film the feeling nevertheless that a bunny bounding in slow motion is silly rather than horrible, it must be because of the rather poor special effects. The most interesting thing about *Night of the Lepus*, however, is the way the object of proliferation is used to tie into a new fear: an unbalanced ecology. Much is made of the fact that ecological balance is a very fragile thing. The movie tells us that when the Australian farmers tried to get rid of their excess rabbits by using poison, the poison killed the birds as well as the rabbits; the killing of the birds in turn caused a plague of grasshoppers, which was just as destructive as the rabbits. Janet Leigh and Stuart Whitman play the scientists who are trying to get rid of the rabbits safely, but even they are not able to do the job without upsetting the ecological balance. The crazily disruptive rabbits, obviously a symbol of fertility, also seem to work as a metaphor for our basic fear of overpopulation. Thus, *Night of the Lepus* depicts another view of the end of the world—an end not by atomic bombs, but an end brought on by ecological madness and scientific-environmental irresponsibility.

Much the same is suggested by 1972's *Frogs*, starring Ray Milland as the ultimate victim. In this one, the cast members are gradually killed by a variety of animals in this mutated ecological niche: there is asphyxiation by smart lizards, bites from poisonous rattlesnakes, attacks from crocodiles and alligators, electric shocks from eels, a successful snapping by a hungry sea turtle, and a heart attack induced by frogs who subsequently eat their victim. Again the structure is similar to that of *The Birds*, with all the action taking place around one main house. When, at the climax, the hero, heroine, and children escape the house and find safety, they are picked up by a passing motorist whose son just happens to have a pet frog. The reference is clearly to the lovebirds in *The Birds* that accompany the Brenners' escape. The movie ends rather incongruously, in the best tradition of American International, with a cartoon frog hopping across the screen burping, apparently, Ray Milland.

Bride of Frankenstein Elsa Lanchester tries her hand at modern horror as the smothering mother in *Willard*

Superstar of Armageddon: *Ben*, rat *extraordinaire*

Perhaps the most remarkable film in this series is the documentary, *The Hellstrom Chronicle*, produced by David Wolper in 1971. The documentary opens with an explosion and beautiful images: water droplets, cell formations, the creation of life. The narrator then tells us that insects, the first to be created, will be the last to survive. Nils Hellstrom, the fictional scientist in this film (played by actor Lawrence Pressman), is constantly undercutting the dignity of man by placing man at the mercy of the insects. One shot pans from bugs in the grass to two human lovers as Hellstrom tells us not to confuse size with importance. Insects, we are later told, can survive the atomic bomb and live in complete harmony with the environment. Only two kinds of creatures are increasing their numbers—man and insects—and in the battle between the two it is obvious who shall "inherit the earth." There is one beautiful almost Peckinpah-like scene of black hamster ants fighting red ants. Another scene shows caterpillars rapidly eating a plant while on the soundtrack we hear the most horrible, augmented chewing sounds. Although it is true that insects have no intelligence, we are reminded that they also have no stupidity; purely instinctual, able to carry on doing only that which has been programmed into them, the insects are compared to a perfectly constructed computer. One of the film's ultimate images is that of a mile-long column of driver ants in Kenya. Discussed in military terms, the ants remind one of Nazis, or at least an insect perversion of *Triumph of the Will*. Truly a horror-of Armageddon film, *The Hellstrom Chronicle* is one of the genre's best. The film has a fascinating documentary form, images of unspeakable beauty that are nevertheless truly horrible, the same interest in proliferation, besiegement, science, and uniformity, and a strong sense of an ultimate struggle which will climax with the overthrow of man.

Certainly the bleakest horror-of-Armageddon film, among the two or three masterworks of the sixties, is that low-budget horror film, *Night of the Living Dead*. As a film it has been much maligned—ignored by many critics, crucified by others. *Variety*'s review of the film was fairly typical of *Night of the Living Dead*'s reception. Almost hysterically, *Variety* claimed:

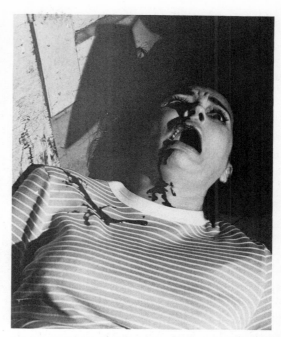

Night of the Living Dead: masterwork of the sixties

> In a mere 90 minutes, this horror film (pun intended) casts serious aspersions on the integrity and social responsibility of its Pittsburgh-based makers, distributor Walter Reade, the film industry as a whole, and exhibitors who book the picture, as well as raising doubts about the future of the regional cinema movement and about the moral health of filmgoers who cheerfully opt for this unrelieved orgy of sadism. . . . Russo's screenplay is a model of verbal banality and suggests a total antipathy for his characters . . . if not for all humanity.

The film originally got in trouble when it was attacked by the *Reader's Digest* for scaring children. In actuality, the attack saved the movie from oblivion and obscurity by elevating it to a position of some notoriety. Nevertheless, although the film has become a cult masterpiece, there still remains the inclination that somehow it is not quite right for it to be so lavishly honored; it is, after all, just a horror film, and a rather cheaply made, often amateurish, and an exploitative one at that. I bring up Ionesco's play *Jeux de Massacre*, translated alternately as *The Killing Game* or *Here Comes a Chopper*, not only because Ionesco himself and the theatre of the absurd seems so instrumentally relevent to this genre, but because *The Killing Game* specifically bears resemblances to *Night of the Living Dead*, which help to illuminate the horror film as well as promote its "acceptability."

Alongside Ionesco's great themes of proliferation and besiegement is the theme of death. For the first time in this play, the themes intermingle directly:

The Killing Game is about the proliferation of death.

> The scene is the town square. Neither a modern nor an ancient town. This town should have no particular character. . . . There are plenty of people about. They look neither gay nor sad. They have either been or are just going shopping

The town of no character is suddenly hit by the plague. There follows a series of scenes with unrelated characters who come on stage, say their lines, and then die of the plague. A housewife says: "My husband told me most of these people have no particular morals. That's why they die. They live incoherent lives." But the good also die. Another man says: "The whole world has become a distant planet, impenetrable, made of steel, remote. Something completely strange and hostile. No communication. Cut off." The plague gets worse. In the middle of the play a character comes out, announces the intermission, and falls down dead; the stage is almost hilariously cluttered with bodies. The dignitary announces:

> Fellow citizens and strangers. An unknown scourge has been spreading through the town for some time now. . . . Suddenly, with no apparent cause, with no previous sign of illness, people have started dying in their houses, in the churches, at street corners, and in public places. They have started dying, can you imagine that? . . . Death is advancing by geometrical progression!

The town is completely enclosed, besieged by Death, who appears metaphorically as a black-robed monk who, occasionally, silently walks across the stage. People lock themselves in their houses, trying to stave off death, but nothing does any good; the evil, the good, the young, the old, friends, enemies, lovers—everyone—dies. Suddenly and inexplicably, the plague stops. The people tentatively come out of their houses and begin to applaud and cheer their own victory over death, when just as suddenly the whole town catches on fire, and the survivors of the plague begin an ordeal even more terrible and hopeless than the one before.

Philosophically, *Night of the Living Dead* is just as nihilistic. Structurally, it works the same, although what proliferates in this film is not the principle of death, but the living dead: dead who arise to kill the living. Starting slowly, the living dead gradually increase their numbers by geometric progression, and when they are quite suddenly vanquished and the hero emerges from his besieged house, the horror of the living dead is replaced by another horror: the inhumanity of the living; the hero is killed anyway.

The film starts deceptively and almost comically. A car speeds down a road toward a corroded

"Suddenly, with no apparent cause, with no previous sign of illness, people have started dying in their homes, in the churches, at street corners, and in public places": the government responds in *Night of the Living Dead:* "No comment"

Judith O'Dea as the catatonic Barb in *Night of the Living Dead:* "The killers appear to be eating the flesh of their victims."

cemetery entrance sign. It is autumn, and the leaves are all dead upon the ground. We meet Johnny and Barb who are visiting their father's grave—for their mother's sake. Barb wishes that the flowers on the grave didn't have to die. There is distant thunder as Johnny makes fun of the church and then starts joking about Barb's childhood "bogeyman" fears: "They're coming to get you . . . Barb . . . they're coming to get you. . . ." The more she tries to get him to stop the teasing, the more he continues, pointing at a very large man who appears to be slowly walking toward them. Instantaneously, the comic tone changes to spellbinding horror as the walking man reaches out and for no reason kills Johnny, and then starts inexorably chasing Barb, her childhood fears suddenly confronting her in reality. She runs to the car and slams the door, but can't get the car started, while the man picks up a rock and begins smashing the car window to get in. The whole sequence is amazingly frightening, but Barb does eventually manage to escape to a little farmhouse (in these films, it's always a farmhouse). She runs in hysterically to look for help and climbs a *Psycho*-like stairway only to find a horribly mutilated dead woman, which sends her into a catatonia she retains for the remainder of the film.

Inside the house she meets the hero of the film, Ben, a young black man. While the house is gradually surrounded by more and more of the creatures, Ben tells Barb almost ritualistically of his encounters with the creatures. Barb's account to Ben of her own experience is disjointed and innacurate; she refuses to believe the truth that her brother is dead. After Ben puts a few of the creatures out of commission, the two of them begin boarding up the house, but Barb brings only useless pieces of wood. When she takes the tablecloth, she folds it carefully, cradling it as if its homey materialism will give her strength—much like Jessica Tandy and her coffee cups in *The Birds*. The radio announces that mysterious mass murder is taking place in the eastern third of the nation; we dolly in to a closeup of Barb as the announcer says the killers appear to be eating the flesh of their victims.

Gradually, more people are discovered in the house, the most important of which is a rather mean, balding, "villain" named Harry, who has been hiding with his wife and injured daughter in the cellar. In the discussion of what to do, Harry is absolutely convinced that they should all lock themselves in the cellar and not come out; he gives a

list of perfectly rational reasons to back up his position. For some reason, Ben disagrees, feeling that it is important for all the survivors in the house to work together and to stick together upstairs. Perhaps because Ben is so obviously the hero, we in the audience find ourselves taking his side, judging Harry to be a sniveling and close-minded selfish coward. The sentiment—"We'd all be a lot better off if we could do it together"—is persuasive, and there is a strong sense here of something allegorical in the black man urging cooperation: a kind of faith that liberalism will get us through. Yet all the personal confrontations are punctuated by images of the creatures sticking their fingers in through holes in the windows, always trying, like *The Birds*, to get in and kill. In the central scene of the film, we watch a news report on television, which says that the mysterious creatures that have arisen and that are proceeding to eat the living are actually dead. There is the fuzzy suggestion that the phenomenon may have something to do with an earthly satellite sent to Venus that was destroyed, but this is only suggested as one possible explanation that quite clearly is not particularly persuasive. One of the newscasters interviews a posse to get more information, and with the remarkable necessity we have to try to reduce everything to logical terms that we can understand—terms that in this instance take the guise of crudely funny slogans—we discover that "Kill the brain and you kill the ghoul," and "Beat 'em or burn 'em, they go up pretty easy." The interviewer asks, "Are they slow moving?" "Yeah," is the answer, "They're dead." Although Harry refuses to cooperate, the group under the leadership of Ben finally agrees that the thing to do is to try to get some gas for the truck so they can make their escape from the house. A young couple, Tom and Judy (who represent, perhaps a bit too obviously, "idealistic love"), volunteer to try to make it to the farm pump. Because of the living dead, however, the gas spills, flows over the truck, and is suddenly ignited as both are killed in a scene that very strongly resembles the scene in *The Birds*, where the birds set the town on fire with a gas pump. Back in the house there is another confrontation between black Ben and Harry. While Ben is outside with the dead, Harry locks the door on him, claiming: "Two people are dead already on account of that guy"—a statement which is actually true, because it was Ben who instigated the escape attempt. Ben forces his way inside, however, and in a rage shoots Harry dead, taking

Night of the Living Dead: Ben tries to ward off the living dead who are besieging the farmhouse.

Harry's body downstairs to the cellar with his little girl. Upstairs, Harry's wife is being strangled by a living dead, but manages to escape. The film suddenly accelerates into an almost unbearable pace. Harry's wife runs downstairs and reacts in horror as she sees that her little girl has died, has come back to life as a living dead, and is now eating her father! The little girl suddenly turns, picks up a trowel, then repeatedly stabs her mother until she's dead. Upstairs, there is the sound of screams: the living dead are now beginning to overrun the house. Barb's brother Johnny suddenly appears as a living dead and grabs his sister in order to kill her and eat her. The little girl then tries to kill the hero, Ben. Ben runs into the cellar, locks the cellar door, and listens as upstairs the living dead have managed completely to take over the whole house. Downstairs, Harry comes to life as a living dead and is killed again by Ben. Harry's wife suddenly opens her eyes, and Ben shoots her. Unfortunately, no description of this scene can even begin to express its horror. The loud screams of the adult audience and the moral revulsion at the thought of a little girl

eating her father and killing her mother are overwhelming. The climax is filled with incestuous violence, suggesting that there is no dignity to human life; that there are no values—only violence, death, and more horror. Even our expectations of traditional heroism are disturbed, for our hero is able to escape the living dead only by holing himself up in the cellar, the solution that Ben (at the cost of everyone else's lives) and even we, as the audience, overtly rejected. Thus, Ben is able to survive the night only because the selfishness and pettiness of Harry has in some strange way been justified, and any faith in liberalism, communication, or human connection, has been refuted.

From this *Walpurgisnacht* we dissolve to a helicopter shot of the meadow area the next day. At first, what we see appears to be more of the living dead making their way across the countryside. A closer look reveals that they are the police "posse," the liberators slowly going across the countryside to shoot in the head any of the living dead that remain. Yet for some reason, the appearance of the liberators is not as anxiety-relieving as we would like. Their crude humor ("Somebody had a cookout here, Vince.") is mildly disturbing, and they carry out their mission with such a plodding rhythm that they seem like zombies themselves. And indeed they are, for when our hero Ben hears them coming and runs jubilantly outside to rejoin a world that is once again back to normal, the men mistake him for a living dead and shoot him dead. The end credits are superimposed over still photos of Ben's dead body being taken away, thrown on a pile of corpses, and burned. Thus even without this one special night of the living dead, the world is nevertheless populated with its own living dead. The nihilism of *Night of the Living Dead*'s director George Romero is as all-pervasive as Ionesco's: nothing survives or is worthwhile—liberalism, brotherhood, family, love, integrity, faith, not even heroism. Certainly the bleakest horror film, devoid of even an iota of hope, *Night of the Living Dead* reflects the underlying hopelessness that marked the social upheavels, assassinations, and senseless violence of the sixties. And for Romero, this absolute hopelessness is the only and ultimate truth.

Perhaps the most interesting variety of the horror of Armageddon is the Japanese cycle of horror films that started in the midfifties and continued through the sixties. At first, this cycle of films may seem to be related more to the *King Kong* type formula, with

The zombies attack in *Night of the Living Dead:*
Walpurgisnacht of horror

Night of the Living Dead: man's existential destiny?

giant monsters wreaking havoc, but careful study will reveal their relationship to the horror of Armageddon. First of all, the proliferation of creatures is not within a single film, but rather in serial proliferation. We start with the monster *Godzilla* in 1956, add *Rodan* in 1957, *Mothra* and *Ghidrah* in 1962, etc. The result of this fantastic series is the creation of a complete popular-culture mythology. The use of the monster in these films is most telling; in the very early films the monsters are fearful creatures. Inevitably Godzilla will come out of the water in a rage, destroying Tokyo. Indeed, Tokyo is partially destroyed in almost every one of these films; and rightfully so; because this destruction is a ritualistic reenactment of the atomic bombings at Hiroshima and Nagasaki. Yet what is important to note is exactly how the atomic bomb is reenacted. Godzilla redefines the atomic bomb in terms of overt animalistic, natural instincts, rather than in

Godzilla (right) and his monster friends in *Destroy All Monsters*: the creation of a complete popular culture mythology

terms of some intellectual "humanity." It is one thing to have thousands of people killed because it has been very coolly decided by men that this mass destruction would ultimately be best for humanity; it is another thing to have thousands of people killed by a natural phenomenon like Godzilla. Thus Godzilla represents the atomic bomb in terms understandable and comforting to the masses. (Indeed, it is interesting to note that the 1956 *Godzilla* is a virtual remake of the 1953 Eugene Lourie film *The Beast from 20,000 Fathoms*, in which the blame for the monster is explicitly put on an atomic explosion.)

One of the most fanciful of the Japanese films is *Mothra*, made in 1962. After H-bombing Infant Island, members of a Japanese expedition find a pair of foot-high twins and an egg. The twins are kidnapped to be exploited. As one character asks:

"We live in the atomic age; are miracles of nature obsolete?" Eventually the egg on the island hatches, and a gigantic larva emerges. The larva then comes to Japan and spins a cocoon against the Tokyo power station. The city tries to get rid of the cocoon by using atomic heat rays, which instead hatch it. Then, from within the cocoon, there emerges the all-powerful Mothra—a beautiful but bizarre, gigantic butterfly. Mothra than proceeds to destroy the city while the charming Itoh Sisters, the ever-patient captives with their sing-song, simultaneous speech, use their telepathy to direct Mothra. Eventually the government decides to give up the twins and, like some airplane of nature, Mothra takes the Itoh Sisters back to Infant Island, and peace is restored. One can see how the mass destruction of the city is related, not to some mathematical, pseudohumanistic intelligence, but rather to the natural instincts of some superanimal reclaiming its spiritual children. There is, incidentally, the theme of beauties and the

Rodan: the ritual reenactment of the atomic bombings of Hiroshima and Nagasaki in terms of understandable animal instincts

Mothra: the egg on Infant Island

beast: the beast of the larva turning quite spectacularly into the prince of the butterfly Mothra.

Monster Zero in 1962 develops many of these ideas even more clearly; especially the idea of mechanization versus natural instincts. In this film, a new monster, Ghidrah, begins terrorizing Japan. Ghidrah is a winged, three-headed dragon, each head with two horns. We then learn that Ghidrah is actually magnetically controlled by the leaders of Planet X; thus he is a kind of atomic bomb in the disguise of a monster. Furthermore, the people from Planet X represent the usual kind of unindividualized mass horror associated with this genre: with their expressionless faces and goggles, they all look exactly alike. *Monster Zero* deals with the question of what happens when men start acting like machines—as one of the girls pleas for compassion and for acting natural: "Man must not live as machines!" Using the same magnetic rays, the people from Planet X also manage to activate Godzilla (the original Tyrannosaurus Rex-like monster) and Rodan (who is a cross between an eagle and a pterodactyl). Eventually, Japan realizes that the magnetic rays controlling the monsters can be

Mothra: atomic rays signaling birth of the new monster

Mothra is hatched by atomic rays

Mothra: an image of horror

Suffering in human terms: *Ghidrah, the 3-Headed Monster*

stopped by sound waves. Once the Planet X people no longer have control, there is a spectacular fight scene in which the nuclear holocaust is again symbolically reenacted when Godzilla and Rodan turn on Ghidrah. Ghidrah finally flies back to Planet X, and Godzilla and Rodan go back to their homes in the sea, more than willing to remain dormant and natural.

Warning from Space in 1963 is much the same, with a friendly planet warning Japan about the danger of the atomic bomb, and then helping Japan repulse an attack from another planet. Perhaps the most interesting of all the Japanese horror films is *Frankenstein Conquers the World* (in 1966) because this film takes the Frankenstein monster, but absolutely nothing else from the archetypal Frankenstein movie. The Japanese Frankenstein is not a

created monster, but a wild boy who has been exposed to atomic radiation. (Aside from its metaphorical presence, the atomic bomb is specifically referred to in almost all of the Japanese horror films.) Running wild in the streets, the mutant boy gradually grows until he is as gigantic as Godzilla. One of the charming aspects of this film is the instant, almost childlike acceptance by the adults in the film that the monster really lives; one of the characters reminds another that he should remember that, although they may have thought Frankenstein had been previously destroyed, it is well known that his heart is indestructible, and that he could therefore come to life again at any time. The fear of Frankenstein is thus the fear of an always-present atomic bomb; though the ideas of a real Frankenstein with a heart and an atomically radiated boy in the city ruins are never reconciled—at least in the English-dubbed version. Both explanations are presented as somehow (though mysteriously) not mutually exclusive. Most of the movie is made up of the gigantic Frankenstein falling in love with a girl reporter, and, King Kong-like, destroying the city and looking into skyscraper windows. The climax of the film is once again a ritualistic re-creation of the nuclear holocaust as Frankenstein fights the earthquake monster in the midst of fire, earthquake, falling buildings, and massive death.

Another charming aspect of the Japanese series is that, once the monsters' destruction is completely understood as the result of natural instincts as opposed to scientific humanity, the monsters become friendly heroes who, positioned around Japan, are even willing to protect the island against attack. Thus in the 1967 fantasy, *Godzilla's Revenge*, the funniest of all the films, a little boy meets Godzilla's son in his nightly dreams and learns to fight by watching the instinctual Godzilla. The film *King Kong Escapes* in 1967 develops the idea of natural instincts versus scientific programming even further. In this reenactment, King Kong is pitted against Mechni-Kong, a robot who is activated through the use of Element X—an atomic-bomb element. Again the struggle ends on top of the Tokyo Tower, with the instinctual King Kong winning over Mechni-Kong, although, of course, the city is once again in ruins. In many of the later films, with their emphasis on the unindividualized alien masses from other planets, there seems to be an undercurrent fear of the Chinese Communists.

Godzilla's Revenge: nocturnal fantasy

Destroy All Monsters in 1968 is one of the series' most epic films. At the end of the twentieth century, all the monsters have been placed on Ogasawara Island (symbolizing nuclear disarmament). Suddenly, the monsters escape and begin massive destruction all over the world: Godzilla in Paris, Mothra in Peking, Manda in London, and Rodan in Moscow. Again, it is people from another planet—this time the planet Kilaak, which obviously represents science—that are controlling the monsters through the use of tiny transistors. Once the Kilaaks' control is broken, there is a final battle between the earth monsters and the Kilaaks' reserve monster. Godzilla, of course, is triumphant, and, as he destroys the Kilaaks' base, Baby Godzilla jumps up and down and claps his claws in proud jubilation. Still, nuclear disarmament cannot be trusted.

By the end of the sixties, the Japanese mythology was overwhelming: their army of atomic forces included Godzilla, Manda, Mothra, Rodan, King Kong, Frankenstein, Baby Godzilla, Ghidrah, Yog (the octopus monster), and Hedorah (the smog monster). The use of mythology has always been to explain away the unexplainable. The use of this cinematic mythology to explain away the unexplainable atomic holocaust and to build from those fears a creative world with its own rules and moral order is an achievment, not to be dismissed as a cheap, popular *kitsch*, but to be studied as a source of a Japanese creative consciousness and conscience.

There is also a relationship between this Japanese variety of the horror of Armageddon and the American *Planet of the Apes* series with its vision of destruction. Unlike most sequels, the *Ape* sequels (*Beneath the Planet of the Apes, Escape from the Planet of the Apes, Conquest of the Planet of the Apes,* and *Battle for the Planet of the Apes*) are not really inferior to the first. Of course the quality is variable, but all five can be taken together as an

Vision of Armageddon in *Destroy All Monsters*

The unindividualized mass in *Godzilla vs. the Smog Monster*

intertwined mythology. While the *Apes* films contain many of the elements of the horror of Armageddon—an object of proliferation (the apes) and, most notably, an overriding concern with the ultimate atomic destruction of the world—their focus is clearly not on the horror, but on the inherent

Destroy All Monsters: the cosmic view of a fragile Earth

A poignant image of the atomic landscape: *Godzilla vs. the Smog Monster*

The Japanese *Weltanschauung: Yog—Monster from Space*

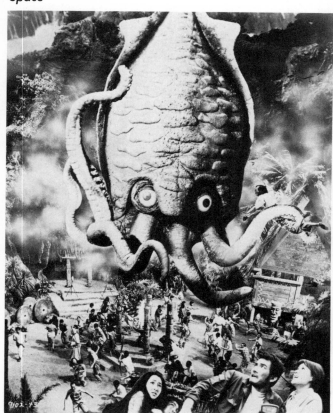

Beneath the Planet of the Apes: Kim Hunter with the obvious solution

The proliferation of apes in *Beneath the Planet of the Apes*

Beneath the Planet of the Apes: a view of the world after Armageddon

Production assistant William Crebar with final revelation from *Planet of the Apes*

intellectual criticism of man through the apes parody; thus, whether the *Apes* series should be included in the horror of Armageddon or in a separate science-fiction category is debatable. Nevertheless, the series is filled with horror elements; indeed, the shock at the climax of *Planet of the Apes* when Charlton Heston sees the ruins of the Statue of Liberty is clearly one of the most horrific moments of the cinema.

Other films on the periphery of the genre include Peter Watkins' *The War Game* (1965), a documentary about the atomic warfare in World War III, called by Bosley Crowther, "a powerful, isolated horror film." Many of the images in *The War Game* are very powerful, especially because of their *cinema vérité* quality: burning eyeballs, people in pain, gigantic explosions, etc. *Lord of the Flies* (1963), based on the novel by William Golding and

Gloria Swanson and bees in TV movie *The Killer Bees*

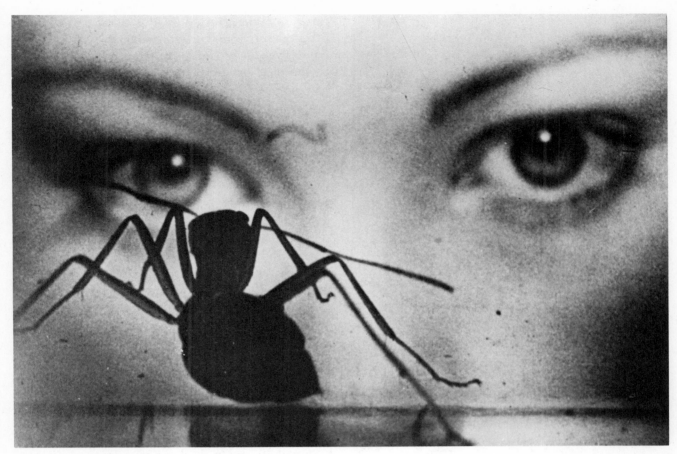

Lynne Frederick becoming hypnotized by super-ants in
Phase IV

directed by Peter Brook, begins when a group of
children crash onto a deserted island while being
evacuated to safety during World War III. On the
island, the group of children gradually reverts to
savagery, reenacting in microcosm the same petty
power struggles and dark natures that brought the
outside world to nucleur confrontation. *They Shoot
Horses, Don't They?* (1969) used the dance
marathon as the metaphor for the horrific human
condition. Both *Village of the Damned* (1960) and
Children of the Damned (1964), as well as Joseph
Losey's rarely seen *The Damned* (1961), used
children as a bizarre intimation of some atomic
destruction yet to come. And, in the anthology film
The 7 Capital Sins, Ionesco's own "Anger" (in
collaboration with director Sylvain Dhomme) is a
clever panorama of a squabbling world that climaxes
with ultimate nuclear destruction. Other films in the
mainstream of the genre include Saul Bass' *Phase IV*
(1974), which deals with invading ants; and perhaps
the most repugnant, *Bug* (1975), which deals with
foot-long cockroaches.

If the horror-of-Armageddon genre seems in any
way to be a limited or transient genre, the remarkable success of *Jaws* should disprove this idea.
Released in the summer of 1975, *Jaws* managed to
become the all-time box-office champ besting in less
than four months such other contenders as *The
Sound of Music, Gone with the Wind, The God-
father*, and *The Exorcist*. Working with certain
generic conventions and against others, *Jaws* provided the new twist that will undoubtedly keep the
genre going for many more years. Based on the
best-seller by Peter Benchley, *Jaws* was directed by
relative newcomer Steven Spielberg, whose previous work includes the Goldie Hawn adventure *The
Sugarland Express* (which garnered excellent reviews and disappointing box office) and the TV
movie *Duel*. The latter, a close relative to the
Armageddon genre, if not a member of the family,
deals with the psychological duel between a
motorist (played by Dennis Weaver) and a ten-ton
truck that tries to run him down on an interstate
highway. The fact that the face of the trucker is not
revealed readily turns the truck into a metaphor for

Phase IV: the beauty of Armageddon

Nigel Davenport during ant attack in *Phase IV*

existential horror. *Jaws* deals with violent shark attacks in a New England resort city, and, as in *Duel*, Spielberg turns his shark monster into a metaphor for existential horror by not actually showing the shark until amost two-thirds into the movie. When the shark does finally appear (in the form, incidentally, of a persuasive mechanical model expertly constructed for the production), audience expectation is so overwhelming and has already invested the monster with such dread that its appearance is invariably greeted with wild screams. Not since *Psycho* in 1960 or *The Birds* in 1962 has an audience so enjoyed being manipulated from *frissons* of fear to heights of horror.

The opening scene of the film shows a group of people around a fire, instantly suggesting the primitive, tribal origins of man. A young man then chases a young girl down the beach in a strangely

timeless sexual rite. With this emphasis on man's primitive urges and primordial needs, the audience is clearly prepared for the horror that is to come; that is, the most primordial fear of all: the fear of being eaten. When the girl is attacked by the shark, the screams intermingle and become ambiguous: love screams, childish screams, screams of fear. Spielberg shifts from this night scene to the beach community the next day: modern, clean, invariably bright, and photographed in pleasing pastels. Certainly this cannot be a horror story: the name of the town is Amity, and it is the fourth of July weekend—a time for independence and celebration, not fear. Yet the shark attacks continue. When a young boy is attacked by a shark and the town is plunged anew into terror, Spielberg ferociously dollies in and zooms out on his protagonist, Roy Scheider. This visual effect (long a favorite device used by Hitchcock) seems to thrust Scheider into the water, literally changing the perspective, forcing him to get involved, even foreshadowing the film's ultimate scene when Scheider, who has always hated the water, will be miles out to sea in conflict with the monstrous shark, and up to his neck in water in a virtual baptism. Scheider is like Tippi Hedren in *The Birds*, who was forced to admit the horror of life and to shed her complacency. Early in *Jaws*, Scheider admits that he came to Amity as a refuge from the horror of New York City with its astronomical crime rate; thus, it is not until he experiences and admits the universally precarious equilibrium of the human condition that he will be free from his fears. Indeed, the final shot of the film, with Quint devoured by the shark (seemingly in two separate bites), finds Scheider swimming almost happily to the shore with a new found respect for the world, mankind, and the water: "I used to hate the water," he says, "I can't imagine why. . . ."

Not surprisingly, the generic resemblances to *The Birds* are extensive. Both films deal with a tranquil and picturesque beach community thrust suddenly into the meaningless horror of animal attack. Just as birds could never peck their way through inches of wood, neither could a shark swallow people whole. The besiegement in *The Birds* of Bodega Bay in general and of Rod Taylor's house in particular is paralleled in *Jaws* by the besiegement of Amity in general and of the ship *Orca* in particular. In fact, almost half the film takes place at sea aboard the claustrophobic *Orca*, with the shark in relentless attack. The only convention not followed by *Jaws* is

The unindividualized mass and inheritors of the earth:
Phase IV

the proliferation of the horror; *Jaws* uses only one shark instead of an army of sharks. This single focus may have something to do with the film's ultimate sensibilities, which seem related as much to the Hawksian adventure film (with the emphasis on men doing their jobs) as to the Hitchcockian suspense film. Yet the horror is inevitably the most striking factor.

Quint, the master shark killer (played by Robert Shaw), is introduced with one of those marvelous touches heretofore called Hitchcockian, but perhaps soon to be called Spielbergesque: the horrible sound of fingernails scratching against a blackboard—certainly one of the most horrendous sounds, almost universal in its ability to provoke sympathetic grimaces. Quint's crude drawing on the

blackboard of shark eating man foreshadows his own demise. Even more telling is the story he relates on board the *Orca* about his wartime experiences the days of 29 and 30 June 1945. On the twenty-ninth, Quint was on board the U.S.S. *Indianapolis* when from San Francisco it delivered the atomic bomb to Tinian in the Pacific, On the thirtieth of July, having completed its mission and now on its way to the Philippines, the *Indianapolis* was suddenly torpedoed three times by the Japanese submarine *I-58*. The 1196 men who were on board tried to survive in the water, but the blood of the wounded and the dead attracted schools of sharks. After five suspenseful days of screaming men disappearing under the surface of the water, Quint and the remaining men were rescued. Altogether over five hundred men were killed, many of them eaten in the water by the sharks. This seeming gratuitous reference to the atomic bombings at Hiroshima and Nagasaki should come to no surprise to those familiar with the genre. Whatever the horror may be—birds, grasshoppers, a shark, or Rodan—the horror seems always to relate in some manner to the A-bomb. There is a sense here, that as in the Japanese horror films, the shark in *Jaws* is Godzilla-like in his instincts. As soon as we hear Quint's story, we know that he must die. The shark is inevitably returning to finish the job left undone that day in 1944 in the Pacific; only after Quint is punished and destroyed (for his role in delivering the bomb?) can the shark be vanquished.

Earthquake as metaphor for the human condition

Earthquake: How soon before the ultimate Armageddon?

Yet *Frankenstein* was never really destroyed; he lived to horrify again in many a sequel. Can this truly be the end for *Jaws*, the biggest box-office monster in the history of the cinema? Or will those jaws inexplicably return to Amity at some future anxious date to wreak more havoc?

Apart from the singular phenomenon of *Jaws*, it must also be pointed out that the horror of Armageddon has influenced another genre, which has made a startling comeback in the seventies: the disaster film. *Airport, The Poseidon Adventure, Airport 75, The Towering Inferno, Earthquake, Juggernaut,* and even *Tidal Wave* (an American alteration of the Japanese import *The Destruction of Tokyo*)—all these films deal with many of the same patterns of endless struggle. The major plot difference, of course, is that in the disaster film the unindividualized horror is not a proliferated one, but one that is whole—such as fire, water, earthquake, etc. A major tonal difference results because in many of these disaster films the resemblance is more to the soap-operatic qualities of a *Grand Hotel* than to the relentlessness of pecking birds. The most important difference, however, is a philosophic one: if, as in *The Poseidon Adventure,* the emphasis is on a similar, horrific *Birds*-like struggle, the films' outcome and sense of life inevitably emphasize the means of salvation and affirm an abiding faith in a basic human ascendancy rather than any existential horror. Thus, the disaster films become the heroic reflection of the horror of Armageddon. The one outstanding exception, of course, is *Earthquake.* Its surprisingly bleak ending has Los Angeles smoldering in ruins, while the archetypal American hero, Charlton Heston, and American beauty, Ava Gardner, are swept down a sewer to meet their horrific destinies. With *Earthquake*, the disaster film copies the horror of Armageddon.

And, indeed, in its essentially existential vision, the too-long-ignored subgenre of the horror of Armageddon illustrates a *Weltanschauung* as consistent and as challenging as that expressed by any *auteur.* From its relationship to the rather elitist and avant-garde theatre of the absurd to its successful box-office status, the horror-of-Armageddon films exhibit a particularly perceptive understanding of that modern cataclysmic corner of our everyday fears.

"You're telling me I should
send my child to a witchdoctor?"
—Ellen Burstyn as Regan's mother
in *The Exorcist*

"Holland, where is the baby?"
—Chris Udvarnoky as Niles in *The Other*

"All of them witches. . . ."
—Book title in *Rosemary's Baby*

Get thee behind me, Satan.
—*The Bible*, Mark 8:33

3

THE HORROR OF THE DEMONIC

Why is the world so horrible? Each of the horror subgenres of the sixties tried to answer that question in a different way. *Psycho* and the horror-of-personality films suggested that the world was horrible because it was insane and therefore perversely violent. *Night of the Living Dead* and the horror-of-Armageddon films suggested that the world was horrible either because man was becoming scientifically antihumanistic or, quite simply, because the malevolent universe by definition compelled the world and the human condition to be naturally and existentially horrible. The third great horror subgenre of the sixties, the horror of the demonic, suggested that the world was horrible because evil forces existed that were constantly undermining the quality of existence. The evil forces could remain mere spiritual presences, as in *Don't Look Now*, or they could take the guise of witches, demons, or devils. Although the high concentration of these demonic films came in the middle sixties and continued through the seventies, films about witchcraft and ghosts have always been with us. Indeed, the idea of an evil incarnate has a long American tradition. The Puritanism of eastern America, with its emphasis on damnation and Antichrists, had as its climax the burning of several witches in seventeenth-century Salem, Massachusetts. The themes of repression and evil forces have long been a staple of American literature, from Nathaniel Hawthorne's *House of Seven Gables* and Washington Irving's "Legend of Sleepy Hollow" to Edgar Allen Poe's "The Raven" and Henry James' *Turn of the Screw*. Of course the tradition of mystic

Julie Harris senses an evil presence in *The Haunting*

evil extends to other cultures as well: the voodoo in Haiti, the East European witches, and so forth.

Perhaps two of the most important forerunners in this genre are *Day of Wrath* and *The Devil's Wanton*, both of which emerged from the spare countryside of Scandinavia. *Day of Wrath* was directed by the Danish director Carl Dreyer in

Hope Lange confronts seventeenth-century Salem in *Crowhaven Farm*

1943. Permeated by a carefully sustained tone of persecution, *Day of Wrath* deals with a young girl's gradual acceptance that she may be a witch because she cannot help herself from thinking evil thoughts. Eventually and inexorably, she is burned at the stake, and the bigotry of her persecutors does not mitigate the girl's disturbing acceptance of her own evil inclinations. This subtle film of persecution, witchcraft, and fear is made even more disquieting by the painstaking photography, which perfectly resembles Flemish painting. *The Devil's Wanton* (although not a horror film), made by the Swedish Ingmar Bergman in 1948, deals with the idea of evil in even less-fantastic terms than Dreyer. Very much a philosophical film, *The Devil's Wanton* suggests that the earth is hell and is ruled by the devil. This proposition is then illustrated by the rather soap-operatic machinations of the plot.

These two different demonic figures, the witch and the devil, returned in the sixties with a vengeance (pun intended). It is not surprising that the rebirth of the devil should come in the sixties; in this period of social strife, any easy explanation for

the problems was most welcome. Further, the election of John Kennedy to the presidency in 1960 signaled a new awareness and acceptance of Catholicism the world round. The early sixties were also the period of the very popular Pope John XXIII; and when Pope John died in 1964, and the Vatican began its search for a new pope, the Catholic church again attracted worldwide attention. Pope Paul VI's visit to the United States in 1965 to make a plea for world peace before the United Nations General Assembly marked the first time a pope visited the United States. Yet, at the same time, while this Catholic awareness reached an all-time high, the percentage of Americans who faithfully went to church reached an all-time low, and *Time* magazine announced in a cover story the death of God in the modern world. Thus, at this point of time, it is not unusual that, while undergoing its sixties' tests of leadership changes, liberal dissent from its young priests, and identity crises, Roman Catholicism, the religion with perhaps the most elaborate mythic and ritualistic ceremonies and structure, should discover so many of its followers leaving the flock and so many people expressing interest in witchcraft: the inversion of Catholic ritual. Thus, because of this Catholic decline, the devils and witches made a comeback in the horror films of the mid- and, especially, late sixties.

The movies in this diabolic genre run the gamut from the most stylized and fantastic films like *The Mephisto Waltz* to the more everyday and realistic *Rosemary's Baby*. Yet the films throughout the

Jesuit professor James Mason and the Virgin Mary in *Child's Play*: Roman Catholicism

The arrival of *The Exorcist*, Father Merrin (Max von Sydow)

genre exhibit a remarkable consistency and tend to share at least four main themes, the first of which is the idea of vengeance. Inevitably, the witches or devils do their work in order to get revenge on people who did them harm in the past. The idea of a vengeance that is compelling, inevitable, and can span centuries recurs in films like *The Haunted Palace* and *Horror Hotel*. In *The Exorcist*, the entire possession of the little girl is carried out, not because the devil has any particular designs on Regan, but, first, because the devil wants to conquer Father Merrin whom he knows will be called in to perform the exorcism, and, second, because he wants to destroy the faith of young Father Karras. The ultimate revenge takes place in *Rosemary's Baby*, where the devil begins his mythically rooted revenge against God for the birth of Christ. The second main theme is the corruption of innocence.

Inevitably, one target of the demon or the witch is a young person, who, if he cannot be corrupted, will be killed. Thus we have the possibily corrupted Miles in *The Innocents*, the ambiguously corrupted Niles in *The Other*, the certainly corrupted baby in *Rosemary's Baby*, and the demonically corrupted Regan in *The Exorcist*—as well as the children that are killed in *The Devil's Own*, *Don't Look Now*, and *The Mephisto Waltz*. Thus, in the demonic universe, nothing innocent can survive: it must be blotted out or perverted. Although, the idea of innocence perverted is not revolutionary (one thinks of *The Bad Seed* or Agatha Christie's *Crooked House*), the idea does contain particular relevance to the period of the sixties; and that is, when children are out on the street demonstrating against wars and espousing political causes, how can they still be innocent? The third theme is that of mystic phenomenon, especially possession. In the world of

The ambiguous innocence of Chris Udvarnoky's Niles in *The Other*

The corruption of Regan (Linda Blair) in *The Exorcist*: demonic possession

the demonic, anything is possible: animals can have human heads (*The Mephisto Waltz*); stone eagles can come to life (*Burn, Witch, Burn*); locks can be mysteriously broken (*The Other*); and matters of life and death can be effortlessly controlled (*Rosemary's Baby*). Accompanying these mystic tricks is the very primary demonic tool of possession; that is, the demon's ability to influence or completely control another individual and to use that influence or control for the promotion of evil. Thus we have *The Possession of Joel Delaney*, as well as the possessions of Tansy Taylor in *Burn, Witch, Burn*, of Miles in *The Innocents*, and of course Regan in *The Exorcist*. The fourth theme in these films is the emphasis on Christian symbology. Demons and witches can

generally be repelled by a crucifix (as in *Horror Hotel*), and some aspect of the church appears in almost every film: the appearance of the Pope and the Madonna-blue of Rosemary in *Rosemary's Baby*; the stained-glass window of an angel in *The Other*; the church scaffold in *Don't Look Now*; and the ritualistic exorcism in *The Exorcist*. The most consistently recurring Christian image in these movies is fire, with its suggestion of hell and ultimate damnation. Note, however, that, although the fire usually kills the demons and damns them with quite proper Christian justice (as in *Burn, Witch, Burn, The Haunted Palace, Witchcraft, Diary of a Madman*, and the "Morella" segment of *Tales of Terror*), this is not always the case: the irony of the final fire in *The Other* is that it fails to damn the demon-child Niles and instead damns the angel figure: his grandmother.

Perhaps the first demonic film of the sixties is *Horror Hotel*, made in 1960, but not generally released until 1963. A surprisingly good film, *Horror Hotel* stars Patricia Jessel, Betta St. John, and Christopher Lee. The movie starts at the beginning of the eighteenth century when Elizabeth Selwyn is burned as a witch. Jumping ahead 250 years, we discover that, because of a pact she made with the devil, Elizabeth has been reincarnated as Mrs. Newless. Our main character, however, seems to be Nan Barlow, a fresh and innocent student who is interested in the occult and who stumbles across Mrs. Newless' coven of witches. When Nan is suddenly killed by the witches, the effect is not unlike the sudden killing of Janet Leigh in *Psycho*. Instantly we become aware that the demonic world is a violent and dangerous one; it is not a world that will respect that popular code whereby the heroine escapes all danger to be united with the hero in time for the denouement. Eventually two of Nan's friends go to the scene to investigate (again, much like Vera Miles and John Gavin in *Psycho*) and manage after a series of scares and close calls to destroy the witches at the last instant by throwing the shadow of a crucifix over them.

The Innocents, made in 1961 and based on the novella *The Turn of the Screw* by Henry James, boasted a remarkably sensitive screenplay by Truman Capote. In this story of a governess who fears that the two children under her charge may be coming under the possession of the dead gardener Quint and previous governess Miss Jessel (the two of whom shared some rather shocking but unspecified

Burn, Witch, Burn: magic

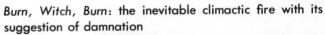
Don't Look Now: the intrusion of religious iconography

Burn, Witch, Burn: the inevitable climactic fire with its suggestion of damnation

Horror Hotel: witchcraft

Christopher Lee in Horror Hotel

sexual relationship), Deborah Kerr, as the present governess, Miss Giddens, hits just the right balance between rational concern and neurotic fantasy. The focus of the film is clearly on the boy Miles and whether he is truly an innocent or a child-demon. Expelled from school for supposedly corrupting the other children by "telling stories," Miles exhibits the most child-like, wide-eyed beauty. Yet, at the same time, he seems almost perversely mature: unlike most children of his age, he claims he doesn't want to grow up; insightful beyond his years, he retorts at one point: "Miss Giddens was just being polite"; his too-long sustained kiss of Miss Giddens is simultaneously childlike yet perverse. The soundtrack of this movie is amazingly dense, creating in the audience a kind of awe and wonder: we hear the singing of birds, the chirping of crickets, the buzzing of bees, the rustling of curtains, etc. The almost heart-rending beauty of nature in this film is sensuous, yet somehow very evil: we see a beetle

Deborah Kerr in the ambiguous and delicate *The Innocents*: understatement

Marlon Brando in *The Nightcomers*: overstatement

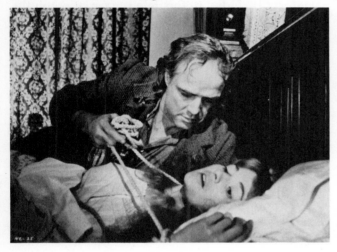

crawling in the mouth of a statue, and the first apparition of Miss Jessel is at the lake surrounded by the trees and the water and the children. Later when Miss Jessel appears sobbing in the schoolroom, the moisture of her ghostly tears presents itself to us as a physical reality that bespeaks an unbearable suffering. When, at the climax of the film, the now-hysterical governess forces Miles to say the name of Peter Quint in confession of his possession, we see the hand of Quint as Miles either faints or dies. As Miss Giddens kisses him on the lips, the night birds begin almost magically chirping. Like most horror films, *The Innocents* works on at least two levels. The ambiguity created by the viewer's constant perception of the two simultaneous levels itself creates both tension and texture: it is never quite certain whether it is the children who

are being possessed by Quint and Miss Jessel, or whether Miss Giddens is neurotically creating the demons from her own sexually repressed psyche.

The density and ambiguity of this film contrasts strongly with the 1972 Michael Winner film, *The Nightcomers,* which is based on the same material, but which graphically shows the relationship between Quint, Miss Jessel, and the two children, before the adults' deaths and the arrival of Miss Giddens. Although the Winner film deals with the same characters and ideas, the horror is of a different nature: by replacing the suggestion and understatement of *The Innocents* with the overstatement of *The Nightcomers,* the horror of such beauty and fragility is transformed into a more direct stomach-churning horror.

The next demonic film was the British thriller *Burn, Witch, Burn,* starring Janet Blair. One of those rare horror films that actually got quite a few very good reviews, *Burn, Witch, Burn* derives much of its scare power from its slow and realistic buildup. In this film, Janet Blair discovers that she has been able to help her husband's career through the use of little charms and magic ingredients. When her skeptical husband destroyes her magic tools, his luck begins to worsen. (It seems witches always try to advance the careers of men: note the piano career in *The Mephisto Waltz* and the acting career in *Rosemary's Baby*.) After the destruction of the charms, the twists then start coming faster: Janet Blair disappears, and when she is found, she tries to kill her husband. It turns out that she is actually now possessed by Margaret Johnston, who is a full-fledged witch. Eventually the house catches on fire, and a stone eagle attacks the husband. The husband manages to escape, but then the masonry supporting the eagle collapses, and his wife is killed. The husband breathes a sigh of relief, unaware that his wife is still holding tightly onto one of her charms. Thus, like many of the demonic films, *Burn, Witch, Burn* ends with a twist that suggests, despite the happy ending, the evil has not yet been conquered.

In "Morella," the first story in the Roger Corman 1962 anthology, *Tales of Terror,* Morella is possessed by the spirit of her mother when she finds the corpse her father had been saving for twenty-six years. At the climax, the father (played by Vincent Price) drops a candle, and all three die in a hell-vision fire. In 1964's *The Haunted Palace*—again directed by Roger Corman and starring Vincent Price—Joseph Curwin, a practitioner of

Jacqueline Bisset and Alan Alda in *The Mephisto Waltz*

Peter Wyngarde in *Burn, Witch, Burn*: the horror of a malevolent universe

black magic, is burned in his mansion in 1765. One hundred ten years later, his spirit possesses the new owner of the mansion. The horror in this film comes to an end only when the mansion is set on fire and Curwin's portrait is destroyed. In *Diary of a Madman* in 1963, Vincent Price kills a condemned murderer and inherits the evil spirit—or Horla—that had possessed the murderer. Varied nasty things follow, including the decapitation of a young woman. Eventually, the reflection of a crucifix awakens Price from his trance, and determined to end the horror he sets the Horla on fire, and they both perish. *Witchcraft* in 1964 uses many of the same patterns. In this one, the Whitlock family of witches tries to get even with the Laniers for taking their land away three hundred years previously. The most important witch, Vanessa Whitlock, is able to rise from the dead when the Laniers bulldoze the Whitlock cemetery. Included in this tale is a variation on the Romeo and Juliet theme: one of the girl Whitlocks (who is not yet a witch) falls in love with one of the Lanier men. The finale is fairly catastrophic; as Amy Whitlock sacrifices herself to save her Lanier love, all the Whitlocks are killed in a gigantic fire, their vengeance foiled. *The Devil's Own*, made in 1966 under the original title *The Witches* and starring Joan Fontaine, is somewhat of a departure from the rest of the colorful films in this period. A British production for Hammer, *The Devil's Own* is a much more realistic film, which finds its horror through everyday observations. The leader of the witches is Granny, a seemingly typically cantankerous small-town grandmother. Again an important aspect of the film is the sacrifice of a teenage girl to the witches.

Yet, in retrospect, all these films seem to be a mere overture to the truly demonic, for the seminal film of the genre did not come until 1968 with Roman Polanski's *Rosemary's Baby*. Polanski, whose previous films showed a very strong influence of the theatre of the absurd, collaborated very faithfully with American novelist Ira Levin, on whose best-seller the film was based. The collaboration proved fruitful: Ira Levin provided the painstaking plotting and careful structure; Roman Polanski provided the visual style and emotional menace. *Rosemary's Baby* is the story of one woman's anxiety-fraught pregnancy and her gradually increasing fears that the people around her are witches who intend to take that baby away from her. Although the ambiguity is not completely dispelled, the ultimate implication clearly is that Rosemary has

Ritual and torture in *The Haunted Palace*

David Niven in *Eye of the Devil*

been raped by the devil and is going to give birth to the Antichrist. This compelling plot is worked out with the most fascinating inversions: Rosemary's husband becomes a demonic St. Joseph; like Mary finding no room at the inn, Rosemary cannot find a place to have her baby; when the baby is finally born exactly six months after Christmas, the gift-bearing visitors to the shrouded crib suggest a dark version of the traditional nativity, the witches then proclaiming: "Hail, Rosemary, Mother of the Devil." As Rosemary, Mia Farrow captures just the right tone of poignancy, appearing at times in the film to be so convincingly weak and pale that the audience almost fears for the actress. Perhaps the most intriguing scene of the film is the dream Rosemary has while she is being raped: like a surrealistic painting, the dream includes the ocean, the pope, Jackie Kennedy, some bizarre creature with claws, etc. The film derives much of its strength from its portrayal of witches, for the witches are not bizarrely mystical creatures, but merely the kind of slightly strange people that we all encounter in our everyday lives and wonder half-heartedly: "I won-

Mia Farrow in the seminal *Rosemary's Baby*

The Stranger Within: Barbara Eden suffers a mysterious pregnancy in a reworking of *Rosemary's Baby*

der what's wrong with them?" Polanski's witches are all fussy and friendly; it is precisely this ingratiating quality that makes them so horrific. Polanski's sense of the absurd remains very strong: one of the film's most horrifying, yet hilarious, moments is when we see the witches through the partially opened door, tiptoeing past almost in parody of traditional stealth.

The denouement of the film, which is very quiet in relation to the frenzied scene of Rosemary running from the witches and giving birth (which comes immediately before), has Mia Farrow tremulously approaching the black-curtained cradle to see her baby; the question as to whether her maternal instincts will turn out to be stronger than her moral precepts is left unanswered. The suggestion, however, is that Rosemary will willingly take on the role of mother to the Antichrist. Polanski's film is filled with the most remarkably sustained tension. Building very slowly but inexorably (like *The Innocents*), the tension arises as a result of the audience's knowledge that something demonic must be going on beneath the surface, even if there have been no dramatically mystic happenings; the horror derives from the subtleties of a glance, the tone of a voice, an unnecessary smile. Thus, from its Biblically mythic foundation to its depiction of a New York in decay, Polanski and Levin have managed to create a truly demonic universe.

The amazing box office and critical success of *Rosemary's Baby* (which included an academy award for then seventy-two year old Ruth Gordon)

94

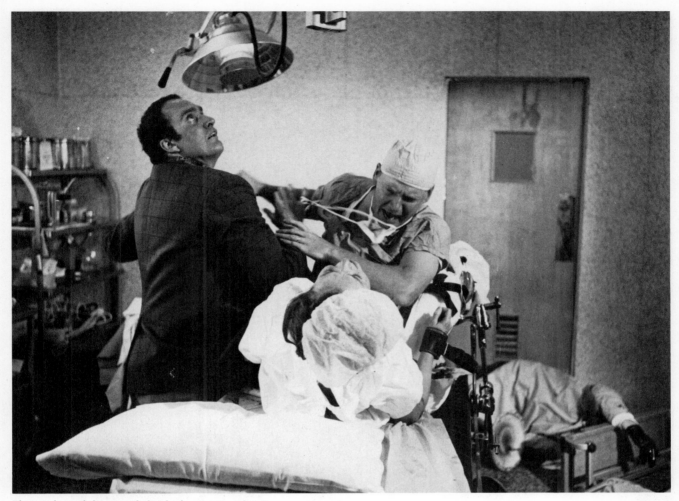

The violent delivery of the baby in *It's Alive!*

spawned a whole series of films dealing with witchcraft, demons, or the occult, many of them with some artistic pretensions like *The Other* and *The Exorcist*. Other of the films were simply blatant reworkings of *Rosemary's Baby*; such as *The Devil's Daughter*, a TV film with Shelley Winters as the head witch; *The Stranger Within*, another TV film with Barbara Eden as the impregnated mother; and the 1974 national release *It's Alive!*, which worked as a kind of sequel to Polanski's film.

"Never Bet the Devil Your Head, or Tony Dammit," a sequence by Federico Fellini in *Spirits of the Dead*, is notable, not only because it, further revealed Fellini's vision, but because it dealt peripherally with the idea of a devil that took as its form a little girl who very innocently bounces a ball, and eventually walks away with Terence Stamp's head. *The Devil's Bride*, released in November of 1968, dealt with devil worship and initiation rites

and brought back Gwen Ffrangcon-Davies as the demonic Countess d'Urfe, the same actress who portrayed the grandmother witch in *The Devil's Own*. Other films of the period included *Night of Dark Shadows*, which was based on the first daytime TV mystic-horror soap opera, "Dark Shadows." In fact, the TV "Dark Shadows," which during its prime attracted millions of viewers who tuned in to the adventures of vampire Barnabas Collins, Quentin, and mysterious Angelique in order to discover the secret of the seven-room dream curse, at one point jumped back in time for a two-month sequence in Puritan New England. *The Blood on Satan's Claw* began with a farmer discovering the remains of Satan in the form of a one-eyed skull and a claw, and progressed to a point where the satanists have an orgy and rape the hero's innocent sweetheart. The independently made *Equinox* used surprisingly convincing special effects of a gigantic blue demonic ogre, as well as a slightly different devil

Night of Dark Shadows: unearthly intrigues

manifestation called Asmodeus. *The Brotherhood of Satan* dealt with a devil cult that was quite archetypally stealing away a town's children in order to initiate them into lives of evil. And *Mark of the Devil*, made in 1970 but not released until 1972, resembled very strongly the film *Witchfinder General*. Originally entitled the very colorful *Witches Tortured Till They Bleed*, *Mark of the Devil* emphasized the sadism of the witchhunter, graphically presenting the burning of witches, the amputation of limbs, and various impalements and decapitations. Polanski's own *Macbeth*, with its strong emphasis on the witches' understanding of fate, thus compelling the tragedy of Macbeth, was equally filled with blood-letting and violence. The obvious relationship between *Macbeth* and the real-life tragedy of Sharon Tate, Polanski's wife, who was killed by the hippie-mystic Rasputin Charles Manson and his family of followers, has been

pointed out as often as it has been denied by Polanski. Yet with its pervasion of a mystically existential fate and almost ritualistic violence, *Macbeth* clearly seems to be Polanski's own exorcism—if not of his personal demons, certainly of the demons of the violent sixties.

The Mephisto Waltz, directed in 1971 by Paul Wendkos, dealt with many of the same elements as *Rosemary's Baby*, but in an extremely fantastic manner. When the famous pianist, Ducan Ely, dies, his soul seems to be transferred into Myles Clarkson's body. Myles acquires Duncan Ely's piano-playing ability as well as Duncan's increased sexual desire. In fact, we discover that Myles had been carefully chosen as the body to house Duncan's spirit so that Duncan could (through Myles) carry on his incestuous relationship with his daughter Roxanne, who, we are told, had at one time literally given birth to a monster by Duncan. Filled with potions, blue liquids, magic books, and satanic

Torture in *Witchfinder General*

The three witches in Roman Polanski's *Macbeth*: the darkness of destiny

Curt Jurgens as the piano virtuoso and chief warlock in *The Mephisto Waltz*

circles, the story is told from the viewpoint of Myles' wife, Paula, who is dismayed by the changes her husband is undergoing. After Paula's child is killed by the witches (innocence can never survive), Paula is so determined not to lose her husband to Roxanne that she learns as much as she can about witchcraft; at the climax, though, she kills herself in the bathtub. The next day when Myles rushes passionately to the arms of his Roxanne, there is the suggestion that Paula's soul has now taken over Roxanne's body. Although the film leaves many questions unanswered (such as: "Where did the soul of Myles go?"), the story is told with such energy and style that the audience doesn't mind. The camera is forever swirling and swooping to the extremely romantic music of Jerry Goldsmith and Liszt, the witches' celebration of sexual performance and passion is compellingly attractive, and the physical colors and textures of the production are always gaudily sensuous. Starting from the same idea as *Rosemary's Baby* (that is, a wife gradually driven to hysteria over her husband's relationship with people she believes are witches who want to harm her child), *The Mephisto Waltz* proceeds with an

Jacqueline Bisset in *The Mephisto Waltz*: the transmogrification of souls

exuberant style that is the complete antithesis of the style in *Rosemary's Baby*. Its consistently downbeat reviews may partially be accounted for, as so many critics insisted on downgrading *The Mephisto Waltz* for not being *Rosemary's Baby*, rather than praising it for its own unique style.

Two demonic films of the early seventies, which might be called the first social-problem demonic films, are *Simon, King of the Witches* in 1971, and *The Possession of Joel Delaney* in 1972. In *Simon, King of the Witches*, the world of satanism is intermingled with the world of drug addiction. Andrew Prine as the Simon of the title, who discovers he has demonic powers and wants to be a god, takes revenge on the world by murdering narcotics agents. In one scene he meets up with no other than Andy Warhol's Ultra Violet, who, as a leader of satanists, does little more than strip off her clothes orgiastically. When Simon's girlfriend dies from an overdose of drugs, and Simon is framed by corrupt police, he uses his curses to plunge the city into chaos. Yet, ultimately, Simon is stabbed to death by drug addicts. One can clearly see in this film the innate parallels between the mysticism of witchcraft and the mysticism of the modern drug culture; it is most telling that, as the almost hippie hero, Prine, is beaten by the "crumminess of the world" and the "system," he becomes a cult satanic martyr: a kind of horrific Mick Jagger or Charles Manson to which the dissatisfied young can relate.

The Possession of Joel Delaney has even more pretensions. In this film, the rich Joel Delaney (who has taken to living in the slum so as to alleviate his class guilt) is possessed by one of his Puerto Rican friends. The Puerto Rican demon, who is filled with rage over the social conditions under which he was forced to live, in turn forces Joel Delaney to commit the most antisocial behavior, such as decapitating his girlfriend, or forcing a well-to-do little boy to eat dog food (to make the boy come to terms with his role as a member of the exploiting class). Shirley MacLaine plays the sister of Joel Delaney, and when an attempted exorcism of her brother fails, it is suggested that it may have failed because MacLaine was not a believer (similarly, in *The Exorcist* in 1974, the atheism of Regan's mother is nicely contrasted with the seeming mumbo-jumbo of the exorcism ritual). If *The Possession of Joel Delaney* seems at times pretentious, it is because it is initially offputting to find in a horror film such overtly applied liberalism and social philosophy; that is, the Puerto

Shirley MacLaine with possessed brother Perry King in *The Possession of Joel Delaney*

The Possession of Joel Delaney: witchcraft and sociology

often manifests itself in these films. Shirley Mac-Laine cradles her dead brother in her arms, closes his unseeing eyes, and then suddenly snaps open a switchblade herself as the Puerto Rican demon jumps into her body in order to continue his revenge against the white upper class.

The next truly important demonic film is *The Other* (1972), directed by Richard Mulligan and based on the novel by (former) actor Thomas Tryon. *The Other*, like *The Innocents*, is the kind of film that is hard to describe: its power and magic residing in its gestures, its glances, its performances, the specific nature of its visual evocation, the rhythm of its editing, the psychological connotations of its moving camera. Like all Mulligan films (from *To Kill a Mockingbird* and *Up the Down Staircase* to *Inside Daisy Clover* and *Summer of 42*), *The Other* chronicles the end of innocence; in this case, not the maturing of innocence, but its perversion. Beautifully photographed in rural America in the era when boys played with frogs, climbed trees, and jumped in the hay, the film introduces us to a pair of twins: Niles and Holland. As it is so often with twins in literature, each twin represents the opposite of the other: Niles is the good little boy, while Holland is the dark brother, the mischief maker. Respecting the integrity of his visual technique, Mulligan keeps each of the boys in separate shots until the revelation that Holland has beed dead for years and now exists only in the imagination of his brother Niles who has taken on demonic qualities. The revelation scene is remarkably reminiscent of the climax of *The Innocents*: Deborah Kerr was positive that Miles would be free of Quint's spirit if only he said his name. In *The Other*, Uta Hagen, as the grandmother, dramatically forces Niles to look at the name of his brother on a stone marker in the cemetery. This idea of release seems related to the Rumpelstiltskin story, where the knowledge of the demon's identity becomes the magical means to the demon's eternal banishment. But in *The Other*, Niles refuses to give up the existence of Holland. In one of the film's most compelling scenes, when Niles is talking to Holland, the camera pans from Niles to the place where Holland is supposed to be; the attempt, for the first time in the film, to unite them both in the same frame is shattering; and what we see, of course, is not Holland, but the empty space where poor Niles imagines his brother Holland to be. As innocent-looking Niles finds himself doing more and more mischief, the effect is quite disturbing. Niles' query,

Rican demon is not to be blamed because he is but a product of his environment; the only way he can get back at the white slave class that has suppressed him is through demonism, suggesting (albeit in acceptable, disguised form) that the crime and violence of the lower classes directed at the upper classes is perfectly acceptable as revenge or as consciousness-raising. Even further, if the Puerto Rican Tonio has now possessed the soul of Joel Delaney, it is only right and expectable because the system has for too long possessed and crushed the soul of poor Puerto Rican Tonio. Yet, even if *The Possession of Joel Delaney* grinds its ax a bit obviously, the film still works well as both a horror film and an allegory of modern class conflict. When, at the end of the film, the policemen kill Joel Delaney, there is one of those fadeout twists that so

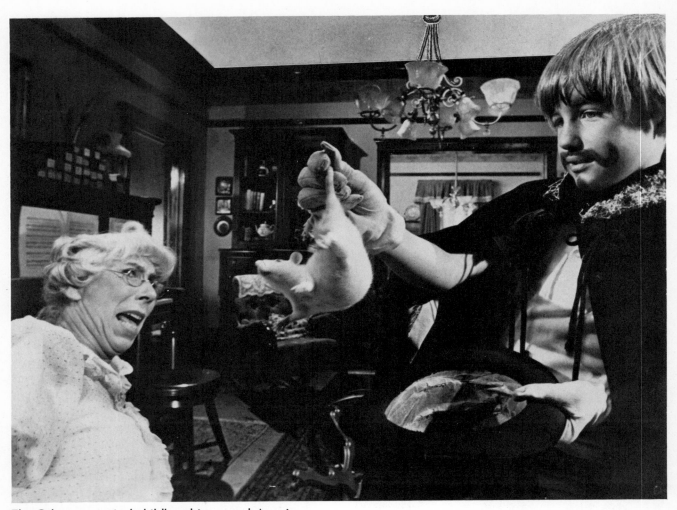

The Other: a magical childhood in a rural America

Chris Udvarnoky and Uta Hagen in The Other: painful revelation

"Holland, where is the baby?" is exclaimed on a wonderfully archetypal night of thunder and lightning above the Gothic farmhouse and precedes the discovery of the dead baby. It is Niles, of course, who is guilty; and, as he imputes the guilt in his own mind to his dead brother, the innocence of his sweet, blonde, wide-eyed features becomes fraught with an ambiguous and horrific beauty. When, ultimately, Uta Hagen decides that she must bring an end to Niles' evil once and for all, her actions strongly resemble the mother's actions in *The Bad Seed*. But trying to destroy that which she helped create did not work for Rhoda's mother either: although the poison killed the mother (in the original book and play, if not in the film version), the demonic bad seed escaped. "Isn't it a comfort," said one of the neighbors to the husband, as the audience realized that the neighbor was going to be the little girl's next victim, "that you still have Rhoda." At the

"Holland, where is the baby?": Loretta Leversee screams in horror as she finds out in *The Other*

Uta Hagen in *The Other* as the metaphorical Angel of Death

end of *The Other*, when Uta Hagen sets herself, Niles, and the barn on fire, she is killed while Niles mysteriously escapes; the three successive shots of the cut lock (derived, incidentally, from the three shots of Janet Leigh's face at the beginning of the shower sequence in *Psycho*) are mysterious yet inevitable, for the evil behind that innocent face is fathomless and indestructible. Our last shot of Niles looking out from behind the curtains in the window defines implicitly the veiled nature of his evil. Filled throughout with wonderful little shocks (such as the hydrocephalic and the fetus in the bottle), *The Other* is most noteworthy for its tone of innocence and horror, its evocation of Niles' youthful exuberance, and its dark vision of the nature of his demonic soul.

Other films of this period include the TV film *Crowhaven Farm*, in which Hope Lange tries to protect herself and her baby from a coven of witches; *Child's Play* (based on the play by Robert Marasco) in which evil goings-on disrupt a boys' school; and *The Pyx*, starring Karen Black as a prostitute who gets involved in witchcraft. In 1973 two of the most noteworthy horror films of all time appeared: *Don't Look Now* and *The Exorcist*, two films that, although not universally praised, were at least treated by the critics as films well worth responding to on an intelligent and artistic level.

Don't Look Now, directed by noted cinematographer Nicolas Roeg, displays an almost mathematical sensibility to horror. An examination of second sight and extrasensory perception, every event and image in the film seems to be related to every other directly and geometrically. The image of Don

James Mason in *Child's Play*

Julie Christie in *Don't Look Now*

Sutherland's little girl reflected in the water suggests a world turned upside down. When the little boy cuts himself, the blood is distinctly red—so is the raincoat and ball of the little girl. When, inside the house, Don Sutherland notices some red fluid emanating away from a red figure on one of the slides on which he is working, it is instantly clear that his daughter outside is dead. The connection between the two events, although "beyond the fragile geometry of space," is compelling nevertheless. When Julie Christie and Don Sutherland go to Venice to recover from the death of their daughter, it is clear to the well-read viewer that one of the two will surely die, for Venice is, after all, from Ruskin to Thomas Mann to Henry James, the city of death, the beautiful city of water and light, slowly sinking to its own destruction. Throughout their stay in Venice, Sutherland and Christie keep running across a child robed in red like their dead daughter. Simultaneously, while they try to get over their grief, a mad killer is terrorizing all of Venice. The film structurally resembles Ionesco's *The Killer (Tueur sans Gages)*. In *The Killer*, the beautiful Radiant City is gradually turning ugly and disgusting as a similar mad killer terrorizes the town. After losing his love, Bérenger is finally brought face to face with this killer who turns out to be a misshapen dwarf, and who, as the play ends, raises his knife to kill Bérenger. In *Don't Look Now*, Sutherland is inexorably brought face to face with his own fate in the same way. After his wife disappears and he sees her mysteriously mourning on a passing boat with two women, he again sees the little girl in the red robe. He chases the girl, and when he gets her cornered so as to see her face, she removes her hood: she is not a little girl, but a misshapen dwarf, the unknown killer in Venice; and as the ugly woman (played by Adelina Poerio) stabs Donald Sutherland to death, the blood oozes from his body just as it did from his slide in the opening scene of the movie. The ugly dwarf as metaphor for the nature of the demonic forces in Roeg's universe is truly fascinating. The cycle is fully completed when in the normal progression of time Julie Christie mourns her husband's death, comforted by the two women on the Venice boat that Sutherland had previously cited. *Don't Look Now* may not contain physical demons, but its exploration of dark and mystic forces is horrible nevertheless. Unfortunately, *Don't Look Now* was widely overshadowed by its brother horror film and cause célèbre, *The Exorcist*.

The mysterious image of Julie Christie in mourning: *Don't Look Now*—"Beyond the fragile geometry of space"

Why *The Exorcist*? If the beginning of the sixties marked a heightened world consciousness of Catholicism, the end of the sixties and early seventies marked a gradual reinterest in all kinds of devil worship. The much-publicized Church of Satan started in the midsixties in San Francisco and acquired branches in many cities with followers estimated to number two hundred thousand. The church's satanic bible, which advocates indulgence in the classic seven deadly sins of greed, pride, envy, lust, and sloth, has sold a quarter-million copies. Other related fields of study enjoying a wave of reinterest include fortune-telling, séances, and magic. It is estimated that there are more than six hundred witches' covens operating in the United States, with more than one hundred thousand avowed witches—and at least half these witches seem to make appearances on national talk shows like *Merv Griffin* and *Tomorrow* and on the various "freak spot" radio talk shows all across the country.

At the same time, we had the rock musical *Hair* with its emphasis on free love and the "Age of Aquarius." Astrology and horoscopes are in; "What's your sign?" is the most common party question. Jeanne Dixon, internationally known psychic, writes a horoscope column and makes widely read predictions. Everyone wants to know about reincarnation, as past lives and future reincarnations are analyzed in national best-sellers. Bizarre violence in San Francisco and Los Angeles spreads all across the country, with messages written in blood and Charles Manson proclaimed a messiah by his followers. And, at the same time, the drug cult, that had been so much into various bizarre ritualistic rites and religions, gave birth to a new movement, the Jesus Freaks, with the result being that some parents found it necessary to kidnap their children away from the youthful Jesus communes. According to many theologians, these manifestations stem from a widespread conviction that the balance between good and evil has been upset in our times.

The Exorcist, which deals overtly and on its one

103

Lee J. Cobb as the detective in *The Exorcist*

Linda Blair, Kitty Winn, and Jason Miller in *The Exorcist*: the precarious balance between good and evil

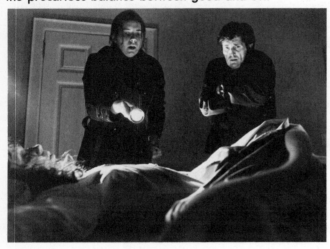

riots, and assassinations—is watched daily over a long period of time on the evening news, and our responses to death have become complacent and anaesthetized, going to *The Exorcist* and throwing up reaffirms man's ability to be revolted, his ability to feel; thus the viewer's vomit almost becomes a valid artistic response to the world around him.

Since almost everyone in the country seems to have been *Exorcist*-ed to death by the media, the artistic value of Friedkin's film seems almost a moot point. Indeed, I think one could easily argue the position that, simply because it dealt with an implicit moral order, *The Exorcist* fulfilled such an overwhelming audience need that it worked like a Rorschach test to which each viewer responded by seeing exactly what he wanted to see; thus, how much of the result was due the film and how much was due the psyche of the viewer may be impossible to ascertain. In fact, when I saw *The Exorcist,* at least a third of the viewers—presumably neutral viewers who were not emotionally predisposed and/or did not feel a spiritual need—found the most "horrific" parts of the film absolutely unscary in every way; and this response came even as other members of the audience were fainting. Whether scary or not, much of the film is pictorially inspired: the Iraq sequence when the priest sees the *malocchio;* the dogs fighting at the demon's statue; the billowing white of the nuns; the flickering light on the bum's face; especially the image of the wind blowing the curtains out from the window, as if the source of the wind came from the demon Regan herself. Yet at the same time, for a ten-million-dollar film, *The Exorcist* shows surprisingly many technical faults: scenes out of focus, reflections of film lights, out-of-sync dialogue, etc. But after all is discussed, there is still innocent twelve-year-old Regan, enthroned in her bed, cursing, vomiting, wiggling her tongue, propelling herself up and down, moving the furniture, masturbating with a crucifix, talking in strange tongues, and killing her mother's friends; in short, doing all sorts of things a well-behaved child should never do—of course, she must be possessed by the devil. The story of *The Exorcist* deals with (as by now everyone except those marooned on the moon during its first six months of release is well aware) the mother's attempts to cure her troubled daughter. A mother's love does not work, nor does the highly technical and advanced godlike science of the curiously soulless doctors. "You're telling me I should send my child to a witch-doctor?" asks

and only level with this balance between good and evil, has managed to reflect perfectly the fears and concerns of its audience: by scaring the devil into them, it reaffirms some absolute, religious, moral order, and provides a hopeful alternative to the audience's religious "God is dead" cynicism. The consistent reports of vomiting and fainting in the theaters where *The Exorcist* was playing (planted at first perhaps by publicity departments?) probably attracted those so predisposed to vomiting and fainting that they needed no more than the title of the film to set them off in fine Pavlovian style. Yet, in some strange way, the possibility that a viewer might faint or vomit was an attractive one; seeing *The Exorcist* was a rite of passage, and only those that fainted or vomited were the winners. In an era where death—in the form of Vietnam killing, live

Karras (Jason Miller) visits his ailing mother (Vasiliki Maliaros) in *The Exorcist*

More possession and exorcism in *Abby,* a black *Exorcist*

Brando in *The Nightcomers*: a reflection of evil

Macbeth (Jon Finch) consults the cauldron: What horror will be next?

Regan's atheist mother. At the climax, after a horrible night of spit, screams, green vomit, and taunts (with the help of Mercedes McCambridge's voice as the devil in Miss Blair), the devil finally gets its revenge on Father Merrin, the exorcist, as Merrin dies of a heart attack induced by the demonic struggle. The devil is now free to exclusively pursue his true victim, young Father Karras, whom he has already tormented by an accusation of homosexuality and by playing upon his guilt over his mother's death, and whose faith has been severly shaken by the whole experience with Regan. Yet the devil underestimates Karras' inner strength; for when Karras realizes that Merrin has sacrificed his life to the service of his God, Karras' resolve is strengthened. Livid, Karras challenges the devil to come out of Regan and directly possess him instead. When the devil does try to possess Karras, there is a struggle, and the devil and Karras plummet through the window. The ending of the film is surprisingly upbeat in implication: Karras' banishing the demon through the Christian sacrifice of his own death reassures the audience that if there is a devil, then there must be a God, and the imbalance between good and evil in our time will eventually be corrected. *This* is the legacy of *The Exorcist*.

Whether *The Exorcist*'s (and *Jaws*') immediate legitimacy of the horror genre will be only a transient legitimacy is not completely clear, but the overriding question suggested by the film's extraordinary box-office success is quite simply: where do we go from here? Before *Psycho* came out in 1960, who would have guessed that a whole new horror subgenre was about to be born? The horror of personality began the decade and thrived alongside the horror of Armageddon. Until *Jaws* rejuvenated the horror of Armageddon, the horror of the demonic seemed to overtake them both. We can certainly expect *The Exorcist* to be followed by a succession of demonic films anxious to cash in on *The Exorcist*'s popularity (*Abby*, *It's Alive!*, *Trilogy of Terror*, *Beyond the Door*, *The Devil's Rain*, *The Reincarnation of Peter Proud*, *The Omen*, etc.), just as we can expect more horror-of-Armageddon films trying to outdo *Jaws*, and an occasional reworking of *Psycho*. Nevertheless, as we now move through the seventies on our way to the eighties, these three horror subgenres are sure to evolve and reveal new formulas, new fears, and new films.

What horror will be next?

APPENDIX 1
DIRECTORS ON HORROR

While the various horror films delight the genre critic with their sustained conventions and archetypes, those same films represent for their directors the eternal Hollywood dichotomy between aspirations and commerce. Without ever denying the artistic merits or integrated patterns implicit in their films (and occasionally acknowledging them with a surprising intellectual understanding), the Hollywood directors invariably view their films primarily in terms of box office, financing, story values, casting, and gambits for attracting audiences. This is certainly not surprising because, for many Hollywood directors, the financial success of a film is crucial; otherwise they may have trouble raising the money to make another. Nevertheless, in the interviews that follow, one finds Robert Aldrich suddenly veering from a recitation of the genesis of his films in order to discuss his own very personal orientation to a world that is filled with unceasing struggle. Genre films (and especially the horror genre) have a peculiar relationship to the Hollywood system: they thrive on it; and their conventions are set as much by the mysterious process by which the public proffers its box-office coin in approval, as by the conscious, "artistic" visions of their creators. The following interviews with five of the important horror film directors—Robert Aldrich, William Castle, Curtis Harrington, George Romero, and William Friedkin—reveal a fascinating view of the realities of the horror genre and offer a valuable contrast to the critical and theoretical considerations that have preceded them.

ROBERT ALDRICH

The office of Robert Aldrich is located in Los Angeles, one block south of the Melrose Paramount Studio. Masculine and tasteful, Aldrich's office is decorated with ad displays of his films and other curios. "I like Bette Davis and I like Joan Crawford," says a matinee matron in a *New Yorker* cartoon on the wall, "But I don't know if I like Bette Davis and Joan Crawford *together!*" Aldrich emerges from his office, a large, jovial, and instantly likeable man who is in his midfifties and has the most remarkably long and owlish eyebrows. In his inner office I choose a large black easy chair from which to conduct the interview, and he chooses its matching overstuffed sofa under a huge and hauntingly evocative oil painting of Kim Novak as Lylah Clare.

How did you first get interested in doing What Ever Happened to Baby Jane?

ALDRICH: A lady named Geraldine Hersey had been my English secretary on *Ten Seconds to Hell* and *The Angry Hills*. When I was in Africa doing *Sodom and Gomorrah* I got this long letter from her and an English publication, *What Ever Happened to Baby Jane?*—a hardback. No one had ever heard of its author Henry Farrell; at least I hadn't. I read it and was fascinated. I went through all the problems of trying to find out who owned it and who the author was. Lo and behold, the publication rights were owned in America, the author wasn't an Englishman but rather a Hollywood screenwriter, and the movie

rights had already been purchased by another Hollywood screenwriter named Harry Essex. So consequently the price for that material had skyrocketed in terms of the commodity market, but I wanted it very badly. At that time the honeymoon was still on between Joe Levine and myself—because he was very happy with *Sodom and Gomorrah* and had already sold a lot of it to England and made lots of money, so he and I bought it together, and we collectively employed Lukas Heller as the screenwriter. Subsequently I wrote to Bette Davis, whom I had never met.

Did Davis have any initial hesitation about doing the movie?

ALDRICH: In those days it was much more difficult to induce Bette Davis to do a picture, and she had never done a picture of that kind before. Davis was a very proud lady about her talent, and rightfully so. Therefore, I was very apprehensive about her

Horror-of-personality director, Curtis Harrington, on the set.

Shooting *Earthquake*, a typical Hollywood studio production; compare with photo on page 132.

Robert Aldrich and Agnes Moorehead on the set of *Hush, Hush, Sweet Charlotte*

ALDRICH: Not on *Baby Jane*. They obviously didn't like each other, but they were totally professional and ladylike. Any comments about one or the other they would reserve for the privacy of their own dressing room when the other one wasn't around. I was very careful and very fair. I had to be objective in terms of getting the best picture. I think it would be unwise to give either of those ladies an edge, but they were totally professional on *Baby Jane*.

It seems that one of your abilities is to cast expertly. Lots of directors engage in the old trick of casting against the grain and then getting applause. In most of your films you consistently cast with the grain and use the actor's own persona as an integral part of the character.

ALDRICH: Many people don't quite understand because they think this kind of casting invades the province of the writer. But since you're in an art or craft that has to do with communication, if the audience through their evaluation of whom the actor is playing the part can understand the character, you can telescope ten pages of the script because the audience will instantly know who the character is, how he behaves, where he comes from, what his background is, etc. I don't say that the other concept doesn't work, but it doesn't for me. In *Baby Jane*, we thought that if you made a movie about the periphery of Hollywood which had something to do with the ancient Hollywood, and put in two stars who were getting old, people would read into that picture a secret show-biz mythology, almost a nostalgia. The audience feels that they are privy to real-life secrets about Crawford and Davis.

How close did you work with Lukas Heller, the screenwriter?

ALDRICH: We're very close. We've done lots of pictures together. You always buy the material first and then do your overlay, that is, you write a long position paper on what's wrong with the material and what you want to do with it. Then you come in and the writer reads the overlay and the material, and then you argue—you pretend to discuss—why you think you're right and why he thinks he's right. The final result is usually a combination of both.

How faithful are you to the script? I get a strong impression that your movies come out exactly as the script has been written, that it has all been worked out with extreme care.

ALDRICH: I think that's true because on those

willingness to be in the movie. So I took a lot of time composing a letter that was arrogant, but I thought necessarily so, saying that if this isn't the best screenplay you've ever read, don't do the picture, but if it is, I'd like an appointment and I'll come to New York to see you. About a month went by and then I got a very long, very polite, but very aloof letter from Miss Davis saying that no, it wasn't the best screenplay she had ever read, but that it came close. She'd be delighted to meet with me, but didn't know if she'd want to make the picture or not. So I came to New York two or three weeks after that and met with Davis and her lawyer. They were terribly hospitable and friendly, and Davis asked only professional questions. At the end of the three- or four-hour conversation she said: "Fine, if the economics can be resolved, I'd like to do it." I don't think I talked to Crawford first. I had already done a picture with her, *Autumn Leaves*, and we had a very good relationship, so I had reason to believe I could get her. We had some billing problems, but everyone was eventually satisfied.

Did the two of them have any problems on the set?

109

Bette Davis and Robert Aldrich go over *Charlotte's* script

pictures we rehearsed: three weeks on *Baby Jane*, two weeks on *Hush, Hush, Sweet Charlotte*. What you see in the film is not necessarily what you see in the script, but it is what you saw at the end of those weeks of rehearsal. In other words, actors—as much as you may dislike them—quite often contribute, especially someone as talented as Davis. "I don't think I'd say that. Wouldn't I say this instead?" etc. Probably she'd say something in between. The script may veer ninety degrees in rehearsal. You also find that it has holes. I can work with Heller because he's English, and English writers don't have the ego problem of American writers. They come prepared to submerge their pride in ownership for the welfare of the project. So they don't mind if at the end of the rehearsal period you say: "This doesn't work, this doesn't structure, go back and in an hour come back with another version." What happens at the end of the rehearsal periods is that you get a refined version of what you began with.

Why after Baby Jane *did you decide to make* Hush, Hush, Sweet Charlotte, *which is basically a variation of the first film?*

ALDRICH: I really had a marvelous relation with Davis and she hadn't done anything worthwhile in between. I had made a terrible picture with Henry Farrell called *4 for Texas*, and he had this other book, not yet published, which he brought to me. I sent it to Davis and she liked it. I thought it would be a marvelous vehicle for her. It really didn't disturb me, it would be different enough from *Baby Jane* so I couldn't be characterized as only a horror-film

director. *Charlotte* is a bigger kind of movie, and the marketplace was very anxious for that kind of movie. In fact, Crawford was originally in the picture. They were counting on the reteaming of Farrell, Crawford, Davis, Heller, and Aldrich, but hopefully it would be better, because the story was better.

How did you decide on using de Havilland instead of Crawford?

ALDRICH: After Crawford got sick, the insurance company had an option to either cancel the picture or give us a short period of time to recast. Our positon was that the whole reason for making the picture was to rejoin Crawford and Davis, so we couldn't just substitute anybody. The only person we could all agree on (Davis, Fox, and our company all had cast approval) was de Havilland and Katharine Hepburn. I had a strong feeling, however, that Davis didn't really want Hepburn to do it, and I knew Hepburn would probably never do it, no matter what we offered her. So I went to Switzerland where De Havilland was living. She had some reluctance about doing it, because obviously she was going to finish second to Davis. Unlike *Baby Jane*, *Charlotte* is really a one-vehicle picture, but she accepted.

The other piece of casting that is exceptional is Mary Astor as Jewel. We are constantly aware of how beautiful she used to be, and the image of Astor now old and bloated is mythically and mysteriously sad.

ALDRICH: I have a hunch that was also Davis' idea, and Mary was brilliant. Our problem was convincing her to do it. She had just published a very successful book and had found a whole new life for herself. Both Davis and de Havilland had been under contract at Warners when she had, and they were very close friends, so they helped to convince her.

In Baby Jane *we finally see that Baby Jane is really not the guilty one. In* Charlotte *we discover that Charlotte is not really crazy. The motif of the character who is in some way a misfit, outside the mainstream of society, who can exhibit more sense and humanity than others, is your theme.*

ALDRICH: Well, I've always thought these people were normal, and the societies outside them weren't. There is a theme I always look for. It comes from *The Big Knife* when Jack Palance says to his agent: "Struggle, Charlie, you may still win a blessing." It has to do with man's intention to try to contain and manipulate his own destiny. It's the struggle that counts. A movie is about what high-school coaches with no talent tell their teams: "This is character-building." And the struggle must change and develop the character. Movies aren't about winning. Football is about winning. Movies are about how people cope with losing or at least try to get a draw in life.

Do you like unhappy endings?

ALDRICH: I don't really. I'd love to do a comedy, but can't get anybody to let me. I'm really a very funny fellow—but no one else thinks so. Most of my pictures have very funny things. I don't look for unhappy endings, but I don't think much of life ends happily. And since I try to make films that are reasonably truthful, chances are they'll end unhappily.

Will you do more in horror?

ALDRICH: I know that I had wanted to do a takeoff—not a put-down—of *Dracula*. And I couldn't get anyone interested. But obviously, now it's too late. The French have made it. Brooks has made *Young Frankenstein*. Warhol even made a *Frankenstein* and *Dracula*. But a few years ago I knew that was going to be the next breakthrough.

I can't discuss horror without asking about The Exorcist?

ALDRICH: I thought I had an outside chance to direct that picture—for about fifteen seconds. Before Friedkin was hired, Blatty had a terrible argument with Warner Brothers and was thinking of pulling the property away from them. I talked to him about buying the property but I'm sure he didn't take it seriously because he needed a lot of money and I didn't have a lot of money. Everyone in Hollywood was disturbed about *The Sting*, because it won the Academy Award over *The Exorcist*, but they shouldn't have, because if they had any brains they wouldn't take the Academy seriously. The two films are not even in the same league. I do think Friedkin blew the movie in the last three minutes though. I don't think the audience understands the interior relationships and the exchange the devil makes; that is, the life of the child for Father Karras. I have many quarrels with the picture, but that may be envy.

And finally, one last question. What films and filmmakers do you think have influenced you?

ALDRICH: I really don't know. I know those are profound questions people rightfully concern themselves with, but. . . . I know I had a million

opportunities. People of our generation spent our youth in the motion-picture theatre. You went to ten movies a week. When I came to California I was very lucky to work with an awful lot of great directors: Milestone, Wellman, Polonsky, Rossen, Chaplin, Renoir, Losey. If you can't learn from great directors when they're directing, who can you learn from? It's like having a front-row seat in a post-postgraduate course in how to become a director.

William Castle, self-proclaimed "King of Horror"

WILLIAM CASTLE

William Castle has become uniquely identified with horror films over the years. While many disdain or dismiss his work as not a serious contribution to the genre, most should be willing to concede that Castle is a filmmaker who knows how to entertain. Castle has a friendly manner not unlike the quality that comes across in his brief screen appearances. One senses in him an unselfconscious desire to serve the audience and an instinctual grasp of showmanship. About *The Exorcist*, he said: "I went to that five times—twice to see the picture, the other times I watched the audience."

(Interview conducted by Dan R. Scapperotti)

There is a sense of "fun" to your fifties horror films. Were you trying to accomplish anything else in these films?

CASTLE: I get calls from all over the United States, in fact I get letters from all over the world, from students who are studying film and have taken these films and are looking for hidden meanings. It's a very strange thing. I definitely feel that possibly in my unconscious I was trying to say something. Many of the films are being taken very seriously today at the universities where they study them. I never expected that they would put under a microscope pictures that I made in the fifties and sixties and look for hidden meanings. Nevertheless, that's what is happening. One of the questions I had from one of the students who called me from one of the universities was: "When you were doing *Strait-Jacket* with Joan Crawford, and she stepped off the train and the smoke enveloped her and just completely fogged her out, was the feeling that you were trying to get that she was going back to the fetus position in her mother's womb? Is that true?" You know, you didn't want to say that actually it was merely that you were trying to make time and the smoke didn't work. And I think about inner meaning: truely, it is possible that deeply buried within my unconsciousness was the feeling of trying to say something. And I get this from *The Tingler*, where they say: "Was it my cry against war and was it antiestablishment?" Many, many times, possibly without really knowing what I was doing, I hit upon a nerve. I think it's very much the same thing they're seeing in W.C. Fields. "Was he antiestablishment?" Well, W.C. Fields was a character and whether he was "antiestablishment" probably never occured to him. And it's the same with Laurel and Hardy, the Marx Brothers, and the little horror films I made. They all have something, and the meanings are far more sophisticated today, and are looked for much more deeply. But that's our audience.

How did the success of Psycho *affect* Homicidal?

CASTLE: I was accused of aping Hitchcock on *Homicidal*. *Time* magazine reviewed the film in 1962 and said it was better than *Psycho*. Whether it was or not is up to the audience to decide, not to me. They said it was a more original piece and more exciting. I must say that in those days I was very deeply a Hitchcock lover, as I still am, and I was very deeply influenced by Mr. Hitchcock. I didn't go and deliberately try to copy *Psycho*, because *Homicidal*

is altogether a different story, but it had the same shocking ingredients. We both had a gimmick, and I think that was where I tried to beat Hitchcock. His gimmick on *Psycho* was a great piece of showmanship. I believe the picture lasted for about an hour and fifty minutes, and during that time no one was allowed into the theatre. You had to wait in line if you came in five minutes after the picture started, or a half-hour, or whatever. You were allowed to buy a ticket, but you had to wait outside. Not until the picture was over was the new audience let in. I was surprised, but the contract between the theatres and the distributors stated this, and it was policed. I waited in line in New York for a half-hour. But I thought this was fabulous, that people actually waited out in line as long as two hours to get in. It was an amazing thing, very much like *The Exorcist* more recently. I felt I'd have to do something to top Mr. Hitchcock and have something more provocative as far as a gimmick was concerned, and I think I did it with my "fright break." The "fright break" was in the last sixty seconds of the film where my voice would be on screen saying: "Ladies and gentlemen, this is William Castle. You are cordially invited, if you're too frightened to see the last sixty seconds, to be my guest and go to the box office and get your full admission price refunded." That in itself was quite a daring statement to make, because there were big houses then with two or three thousand people. And outside we actually refunded money at the last minute at a display we called "The Coward's Corner." Very few people did go out, some just to see if we would indeed pay the admission price, and others would leave their girlfriend or boyfriend in the theatre and collect the one admission. But in a full house it was one percent at most.

In comparison to your earlier horror films, Homicidal *seems to be more sophisticated. Were you striving for something more than just scaring your audience?*

CASTLE: Oh yes. I was growing up at the time. You know, as one grows and does more and more films, one becomes a little more sophisticated. I was trying really to do a shocker on an intellectual plane.

Eugenie Leontovich and Jean Arless give fascinating performances in the film. Did you consider trying to get bigger names?

CASTLE: I didn't have the money. That is the reason I associated myself so closely with my own films. I was the star because I had no choice. I had to have somebody that I could get before the public.

How do you feel about the success of the two Arless personas in the film?

CASTLE: That's very interesting and a whole story in itself. That would make a book. I wanted to use a complete unknown because if any of the audience recognized the character that was playing the two parts it would spoil it because they would then know it was either a man or a woman. I got a girl who was completely unknown and I changed her name to Jean Arless. I made up the name Jean because it's ambiguous, you don't know whether it's a boy or a girl. I transformed this girl, who was a very beautiful girl, into a boy. We cut her hair, we had false appliances made for her mouth to change its structure, we changed her nose, and did everything we could to give her face a masculine appearance. She did all the scenes involving the boy first, and, in effect, became the boy off-screen as well as on it, and then did a transformation as the girl. She wore a wig over the cut hair, becoming a very feminine, delightful, lady. The two parts of her—the two ids—were constantly at war with one another. It took a long time for this girl to get over this double transformation, and for a long time she didn't know what she was. People didn't know. Even to this day when they see the picture on television or in a rerelease, they'll ask if it were a girl or boy. At the end of the picture, you'll remember, I had *her* come out and had *him* come out on a split screen, and they bowed to each other and bowed to the audience for a curtain call.

Was that double curtain call your idea?

CASTLE: Yes. And people would argue outside, was it indeed a girl or was it a boy? And I had a lot of fun with that because I never really told what it was.

Strait-Jacket *seems to show the influence of* What Ever Happened to Baby Jane? *To what extent were you influenced by that film?*

CASTLE: I was influenced by it. I think that Bob Aldrich is a very fine talent. I saw *Baby Jane* and I was amazed at the business it was doing, how good the film was, and at seeing two great superstars playing in this shocker. It was just an amazing phenomenon. I saw it three or four times and I said I must do a film with either de Havilland or Davis or Crawford. I developed *Strait-Jacket* from an idea of my own. While it was in no way the same story, we used Crawford. The film, I think, did more business

than *Baby Jane*. It was one of my most successful films.

In Strait-Jacket *we have what appears to be one of your favorite devices—the hatchet murder. Are you particularly fond of this?*

CASTLE: No. As a matter of fact, where else is it shown in any of my pictures?

In House on Haunted Hill *you have the woman using an axe.*

CASTLE: Oh yes. It's always a good gimmick, you know. For *Strait-Jacket* I got the springboard from Lizzie Borden. From the Lizzie Borden murders I devised a woman and her problem with that axe. I'm not axe-happy.

The career of Joan Crawford was somewhat revitalized by What Ever Happened to Baby Jane? *How was Crawford to work with on* Strait-Jacket?

CASTLE: Oh God, Joan Crawford is one of the great, great stars of any time. She is disciplined, she is dedicated, she is marvelous to work with. She's the best star I've used in any of my pictures, outside of Vincent Price. I resurrected his career too. It was starting on *House on Haunted Hill* and during *The Tingler* that got him going with the American International Pictures. He's never stopped since then. But getting back to Crawford, I did another film with her as soon as I could, a picture that I like and one of my best: *I Saw What You Did.*

Do you feel that crazy people are more horrifying than monsters like Frankenstein?

CASTLE: Not necessarily. It's a different technique. One is horror, the other is shocker. Of course, I have my own definition of horror, and I have my own definition of the thriller. Hitchcock makes thrillers (or shockers). I make both. A horror picture is taking a monster and having the audience scream or be frightened by this monster—*Godzilla, The Creature from the Black Lagoon.* A thriller or a shocker involves an identifiable person that you might be—a girl in jeopardy, or somebody in trouble—that the audience roots for or identifies with. So there is a difference between the thriller or the shocker and the horror piece. I get very frightened of people rather than monsters. I think people are more fun to work with than monsters anyway.

Joan Crawford in a scene from *Strait-Jacket*

CURTIS HARRINGTON

Curtis Harrington lives in Hollywood Hills in a nicely decorated house furnished wisely and in good taste. On the wall is a French movie poster for his film *Games*, which reads *Diable à 3 (The Devil at 3)*. Harrington himself is a pleasant, friendly person whose films exhibit a certain nostalgiac sense of the macabre. He has worked ably in the horror-of-personality genre, and more consistently than any other director.

(Interview conducted by Dale Winogura and Stuart Kaminsky)

Do you think you are a typed director, typed as a director of mental anguish?

HARRINGTON: In the eyes of the motion-picture industry, such as it is, I am probably "typed" as a director of horror films and thrillers. The concept "director of mental anguish" is one that I'm afraid most producers in Hollywood wouldn't understand.

What has been the extent of your involvement with your films?

HARRINGTON: *How Awful About Allan* was offered to me by George Edwards and Aaron Spelling. *What's the Matter with Helen?* was a project I was deeply involved in from the time it was just a gleam in Henry Farrell's eye. It was Farrell's original story and screenplay, but it was absolutely a project that I was instrumental in bringing about.

How much of the writing do you do on your films?

HARRINGTON: I contributed conceptually to some of the writing of *What's the Matter with Helen?* I co-wrote the original story of *Games*. The amount of writing I actually do varies tremendously from project to project. My preference is to work very closely with a writer on the development of a film that I want to do, since I do not consider myself to be a first-class writer—especially of dialogue, which I consider to be a special skill.

In Games *and* What's the Matter with Helen? *would you say that you were working within and against*

Curtis Harrington on the set of *Games*

genre conventions at the same time?

HARRINGTON: It's hard for me to think of them in those terms because I'm really more interested in using the genre to express my own interests. In *Games*, for instance, the whole concept goes back to what Henry James wrote, in which underlying it all is the story of the contrast between European decadence and American innocence. These are the elements I like to work with. As far as I'm concerned, I have yet to make a horror film. I would like to make one. Horror films are usually of a more fantastic genre, in the tradition of Frankenstein and Dracula. Those, to me, are true horror films. What I have made are really psychological mystery stories. Certainly I'm not unaware of the debt that *Games* owes to *Diabolique*. There are elements of horror in those films; I just wouldn't call them horror films.

Games: emphasis on set design

115

The whole idea of *Games* really came about because of my intense admiration for the work of Josef Von Sternberg (*The Blue Angel, The Devil is a Woman, Shanghai Express, Anatahan, Blonde Venus*). I very much wanted to create a latter-day vehicle for Marlene Dietrich at the time. The only reason why she didn't play it was that the heads of the studio simply would not entertain the thought of her even being in it. I was never even allowed to present the script to her. They felt she was not a star of current enough importance, whereas Simone Signoret was still considered to be much more of a current star.

There is a rich, granular texture to Games *that is very well realized. How was this achieved?*

HARRINGTON: I had the good fortune to work with William Fraker, who is in many ways my favorite of all the cameramen I've worked with. This was his first film. Before this he was an assistant cameraman. Despite my visual orientation, I'm not a director who can tell the cameraman where to put the lights, but I certainly tell him in essence what I want, then he can technically achieve it. The better the cameraman is, the less I have to say to him, and that was certainly the case with Bill Fraker.

There was a diffused quality to the film. Was that done with both diffused filters and lighting?

HARRINGTON: Yes. We chose that as the style. I used that effect again very consciously in *The Killing Kind*. We used a Harrison fog filter on most work of greater or lesser density. In *Games*, it was portraying a kind of enclosed, hothouse world in which these people lived. *The Killing Kind* is my most realistic film; even though it deals with murder and obsessive personality, it really deals with the everyday. There is no exoticism in it whatsoever. There, I was trying to make an overall comment on the whole thing, which is ultimately, in a way, a kind of nightmare. I wanted that slight removal from reality to put you in a more subjective world.

What conscious connections do you find between Games *and* Diabolique?

HARRINGTON: Certain plot devices are the only main connections between the two. I wanted to do a story that would seem like a fantasy about a supernatural visitation that would be revealed as a hoax at the end, which was exactly what *Diabolique* was.

How do you feel about What's the Matter with Helen?

HARRINGTON: To me, the film was a very affectionate re-creation of a period in Los Angeles history, which I have my own tremendous feelings of nostalgia for. I was trying to show lives on the fringe of Hollywood in the thirties, not within the industry. I had tremendous feelings of sympathy for both characters in the story.

You never have all-white, all-black characters in your films. Like Hitchcock, you work for the shades of gray.

HARRINGTON: That to me is very important because I try to make my characters real rather than something that is a matter for the author's convenience. Ambiguity of character and situation is something that intrigues me. I would love to do more Pirandellian themes because they fascinate me.

How do you feel about the similarities in plot structure of the horror-of-personality films, including your own?

HARRINGTON: I do not look for such similarities, so these are the things that are after the fact. I think you find in the work of a great many artists that, in essence, they tend to say the same thing over and over again. This is not a bad or negative thing. It is up to the critic to attach whatever importance he wants to them. These may be unconscious resonances, and I think it is bad for anyone who works creatively to become aware of all this. I've always felt it was wrong for an artist to be psychoanalyzed. The one or two times that I've failed is when I've worked out something intellectually. I have to have a kind of gut feeling about what I'm doing, and just follow that.

Your sense of nostalgia is strangely inverted. You're affectionate towards it, and yet rather critical of it. It can be comforting to live in the past, but also dangerous and even tragic, as What's the Matter with Helen? *and* The Killing Kind *show.*

HARRINGTON: That was very much in Signoret's character in *Games* also. The whole nostalgia thing was ruthlessly used by her to pull that girl in. In the trunk scene, when she pulls out mementos from the past, she is using nostalgia to create a certain impression. My nostalgia is really for periods in which I didn't live at all. I feel no nostalgia at all for the forties, when I was young.

Did you choose the title for Who Slew Auntie Roo?

HARRINGTON: No, certainly not. The film, while in production, was called *The Gingerbread House*.

Debbie Reynolds and Shelley Winters in *What's the Matter with Helen?*

Shelley Winters and Mark Lester in *Who Slew Auntie Roo?*

This was an appropriate title and it was the title I gave the script. *Who Slew Auntie Roo?* was the producers' idea of a commercial title. It is my opinion that it harmed the commercial chances of the film. There is one cut in the film that was imposed by the producer: the abrupt end of the confrontation scene between Auntie Roo and her servant. I also did not approve of the casting of the actor who played the servant. That was also imposed by the producers.

How did this project develop?

HARRINGTON: I was approached by American International to do the film. Also, Shelley Winters, who had worked with me on *What's the Matter with Helen?*, asked for me to direct her in it. It was not a project that I personally wanted particularly to do.

Did you write any of it?

HARRINGTON: I did no actual writing on the film, though I did suggest some of the plot elements; especially the idea of Auntie Roo keeping the mummified body of her dead child, having been unable psychologically to bury her. Gavin Lambert contributed quite a bit of the dialogue. The first draft of the script was laid in the present day, and it was my idea to place it in the early twenties. I have a great fondness for all the imagery and quality of the traditional Victorian Christmas celebration. I tried to put as much as I could of that in the film. It was just a rather thin little fable. I found Shelley Winters' mad behavior vastly amusing. I do feel that I achieved the pathos of the situation at the end. There are an awful lot of moments in it that are purely filmic that I did on the set.

Where did you find the sinister house in which Auntie Roo lives?

HARRINGTON: The house was a real house at Shepperton Studios that ordinarily is used there as the main administration building. The facade of the house was completely revamped for the film by art director George Provis.

Your concern with complex detail is striking, especially in Auntie Roo *and* Helen. *How much attention do you personally pay to art direction?*

HARRINGTON: I give a great deal of attention to art direction and set direction. I am personally concerned with every prop. I give my people a general idea of what I want, then if I don't see what I want, I become even more specific.

How long did it take you to shoot Auntie Roo, *and how much did it cost?*

HARRINGTON: We had a forty-day shooting schedule. I don't know the final cost, but I imagine it to be around $800,000.

You seem to work particularly well with Shelley Winters.

HARRINGTON: We seem to understand each other. She is sometimes a difficult, headstrong actress, but she is also extremely talented. She makes wonderful "choices" as an actress, and has an unerring sense of dramatic truth. The little displays of temperament are easy to cope with when you know you are getting something worthwhile on the screen.

Are you satisfied with Auntie Roo?

HARRINGTON: I'm not wholly satisfied with any film

I've made. I feel that I did just about the best I could do with *Auntie Roo*, however, under the circumstances. When I was younger, I felt that by the brilliance of style alone, a director could transform anything. I don't believe that anymore. You've got to have something to work with. This was brought home to me especially in relation to *Who Slew Auntie Roo?* It had a very weak, incredibly lousy script. Believe me, what I finally shot is an incredible improvement over the original. Even so, it was very difficult to do enough with it to make it work. I was also saddled with a very bad cameraman that I couldn't control. I still think that whatever flaws it had, it turned out astonishingly well, considering that it was a terrible uphill struggle for me all the way.

GEORGE ROMERO

When Continental Films dumped *Night of the Living Dead* onto the summer/fall drive-in circuit in 1968 with a typically gross exploitation campaign, who could have expected that this cheap, black-and-white horror film was anything more than what it appeared to be? Director George Romero is one of the film's makers chiefly responsible for its unexpected intelligence and sophistication.

(Interview conducted by Tony Scott)

Do you have any special interest or fondness for making "horror films?"

ROMERO: I didn't in the beginning. When we made *Night of the Living Dead,* we made it as our first picture, and our friends in distribution circles told us to make something exploitive because it's safer. So we decided to do a "horror film." Now when we did it, we said, we're not going to do just a horror film, we're going to really go out with it and try to make it "gutsy." I have a theory that there are so many films that haven't been done, that *have* been done a hunded times, but haven't been done yet. One of them for example, is *Tarzan of the Apes.* Because it hasn't been done yet. I'd like to do it exactly the way Burroughs wrote it, and I think it would be a tremendous piece of a Victorian kind of escapism.

How long have you been based in Pittsburgh?

ROMERO: I came out here to go to school at Carnegie Tech to study painting and design and Spanish background. I'm influenced by the Spanish paint-

George Romero, behind camera, shooting a scene from *Night of the Living Dead*

ers. I think that perhaps my approach to the visualization of something comes out of that rather than any influence from any director or cinematographer that I've studied.

I think that may be what gives the film that Romero touch.

ROMERO: I think that anyone who has an eye for composition or the translation of anything to a two-dimensional format is influenced by two-dimensional things that he's seen, not so much by film. No matter how many times you watch a film, you may see any given shot for a matter of, in the aggregate, two or three minutes, whereas you can look at a painting or a graphic that you have in your home, something that you really like, endlessly.

How did you develop the theme of Night of the Living Dead?

ROMERO: I wrote a short story which was in fact an allegory, a statement about society which dealt with a siege by the living dead. It was much less contrived than the film is, from the standpoint that it was purely allegorical. Now a lot of the people that have

Special-effects preparation on *Night of the Living Dead*

seen the film are seeing the allegory coming out of the film anyway.

I've heard it called a political film.

ROMERO: That was in my head when directing it, when we were looking for an approach to it, but I don't think it is really reflected in the film.

Did you have any trouble with the cast and crew, getting them to take the film seriously because it was a horror film?

ROMERO: Not really, no. Of course we've always had a pretty good group of people. We have a totally in-house unit. We work with each other well. We know what our intentions are and we don't have any internal strife or anything like that—so we have a pretty good time. You have fun no matter what you're doing. You can be doing *Hamlet* and I think you'll have fun doing it.

Did you have any trouble getting money or backing for the actual production of Night of the Living Dead?

ROMERO: Yes. It was our first time out and Pittsburgh is a very wealthy city, but it's the kind of money that's in Pittsburgh; it's not gambling money; it's nuts-and-bolts industrial money. It's very difficult. When we first went around, we tried for about three years before we made *Living Dead* to get people to fund some kind of a project, thinking all along that we were going to do a serious piece. In fact, we had a script that I had written that we were trying to promote. We had an entire package put together and we couldn't get any cash here and we tried to get cash in New York. People were interested in the script, but they wanted to buy it, take it away, and make it. We said no, our idea is to make the film. When we told people here in Pittsburgh that we were going to make a feature film that was going to be released, they would say, "Uh huh, oh yeah. . . ." and walk away. That was that. We just couldn't do it. We finally formed another corporation. There were ten of us, and the corporation was called Image Ten. We each put in a little bit of seed money, which was enough to buy our film stock, and we talked to the cast on the basis of deferred payments. The cast agreed and we started to shoot; but of course we were still doing commercial and industrial films. Therefore, *Living Dead* was shot over a period of nine months with great breaks in between to come back and do a pickle commercial or something, which was distressing. After we got some footage in the can where we could screen rushes for people, people started coming around saying, "Hey, that looks like a movie!" and we said, "Well, that's what it is!" And they said, "Oh yeah . . ." and finally started to put up money.

How would the film have been different if it had been made by AIP in Hollywood?

ROMERO: I think that there probably would have been a scientist in the group, explaining what was going on. I think the ending would have been different. In fact, American International turned the picture down on the basis of it being too unmitigating. They told us that if we would reshoot the ending they would distribute it; that is, have Ben survive.

Do you feel that comedy is appropriate in horror films? Hammer Films very seldom have humor. Does it make it almost camp when it's too serious?

ROMERO: I think it does. Hammer films have excellent production values, they have a tremendous feel for that Gothic aura, they have good people,

Cast of *Night of the Living Dead* poses with the black paint and Bosco used for blood in the film

good actors, but there is something about their films that is just . . . stiff upper lip, and every damn one is exactly the same. They're all kind of on one line, and you never get off it. There's material in *Living Dead* that gets a kind of nervous laughter. I know Hitchcock has a philosophy: he will always follow a very tense sequence with a little piece of comedy. He does it all the time. If you study his work, it works very well. In *Living Dead* we have a couple of instances like that. Right in the middle of the uptight-thing with the posse, the sheriff is saying some very funny things. I don't think it's counter-productive at all.

Does it bother you when you're in an audience with your own film, and the audience reacts differently than you expected them to?

ROMERO: No. I always find it interesting. I really think that anyone that endeavors to do anything creative is really trying to communicate, and reaching people in any way is a substantial thing. When I was acting I did a play called *The Connection* and played a character named Leach. I had to come down center stage and take a needle in the arm and take an overdose and then go into fits with my arm hanging off the proscenium with the needle hanging out of the vein. We did it with nose putty. And every night it was a different reaction. It was really a tremendous thing. We got nervous laughter to that,

we got some cringing, we got some people in nausea—and you know you're doing something. That's a gratifying thing. I've seen *Night of the Living Dead* with audiences three or four times. It has, pretty much, a uniform reaction.

Your most recent production is The Crazies . . .

ROMERO: The original title was *The Mad People*, and I liked that better. That film also was originally written as a pure allegory; the basic premise being that everyone in the world is opeating at some level of insanity. You know, the old question, what is sane, what is insane? The device that was used in the story was the accidental spill of a biological weapon into the water supply of a little town. In the original version, the romantic leads were to get separated. Nobody knows what's going on. Suddenly the military moves in and—bang!—they're all over the place. They want to contain the virus caused by the seepage into the water supply. The whole time there's a bomber over the town because of the possibility of the virus being carried out; there's the chance that they may have to bomb the town. We were going to end it with the two lovers, after having been separated, running toward each other and just before they reach each other on the screen, the screen was going to go white and the military were going to destroy the town with the bomb. But we didn't do that.

WILLIAM FRIEDKIN

As Bill Friedkin sat in his eighth-floor suite at the Continental Plaza Hotel in Chicago drinking coffee and fielding questions, he conveyed the impression of a young man confident enough in his craft that pretentions and defenses were not necessary. He began his career in the mailroom at WGN-TV in Chicago. Within two years he was directing live TV, which led to documentary films and eventually an entry into feature-film directing. In his midthirties and clad in corduroys and open-neck shirt, Friedkin occasionally adjusted his wire-rimmed glasses as he spoke quite candidly about *The Exorcist*.

(Interview conducted by Bill Crouch)

FRIEDKIN: Strange as it may sound, I tried not to make a film about Satan. *The Exorcist* is more about expectancy set, the mystery of faith, the mystery of goodness. What it is to me is a realistic film about unexplainable things. I personally have no strong

William Friedkin directing Ellen Burstyn in *The Exorcist*

conviction about Satan or a personified devil. I have no strong conviction against that either, but I didn't want to make a film that pushed that. There is a very solid underpinning in the film for any other explanation that one may wish to gather, but I take it that not too many people want other explanations.

Were you surprised about the strong reaction the film evoked from many?

FRIEDKIN: On the front pages of newspapers there are pictures and stories about people being led out of the theatre on stretchers, or running out screaming, fainting, vomiting. All over the country I've gotten calls from radio stations asking me how I feel about that. I'm shocked that that happened. I thought that people might be moved by the film. I never thought they would become hysterical or start screaming or fainting. That was never in my wildest imagination. I

can't understand, I don't know what to say about that.

What do you see as the purpose of the prologue or the Iraq scene of the film?

FRIEDKIN: The Iraq scene introduces to you what kind of man Father Merrin is, the man who is called in as an exorcist. It establishes, in a kind of abstract fashion, that Merrin gets a premonition that he is going to have to perform an exorcism. It also establishes the fact that he is not a very well man. That he is a very sick man. And this sick old man, who is given to believe in omens and symbols, is going to be asked to drive a demon out of a little girl. It's a terrific device that was in the novel. I remember Blatty telling me that at one point his publisher asked him to cut it out of the novel. He did take it out before the book went to publication, and then he missed it because he realized that it sets the tone for the whole thing. It starts the thing out on a

121

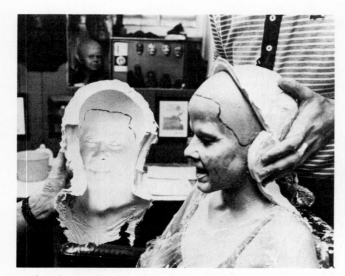

Linda Blair and plaster cast

kind of strange mysterious level. It's not apparent why you're seeing it, but later when you think about it, it all becomes clear. So I used it to foreshadow things visually that occur later. For example, in my mind, the picks that you see being pushed into the ground foreshadow the crucifix being driven into the girl's vagina. The dirt oozing out in several shots foreshadows the vomiting. And I clearly shot every sound and sequence to foreshadow something that you see or hear later. Another example of this is the blacksmith sequence. The anvil sound is in the exorcism, and the blacksmith who only has one eye, his eye resembles the little girl's eyes when they go up into their sockets.

Are there any aspects of the film which you conceived as having larger symbolic implications?

FRIEDKIN: Well, I should say that I know what things were in my head when I shot the film. I really couldn't tell you what anything means on a more symbolic level. I never got out of high school! But I do know that the prologue was intended as visual metaphor. I tell stories with pictures, and I have these visual metaphors that have meaning to me, but I don't know what they mean to you. They aren't deep, for God's sake. Jodorowsky uses very difficult and meaningful psychological and religious symbols in his movies. I have no training in religion or psychology and I'd be a fool to try to put that sort of thing in. But I do try to put in visual metaphor. In the early days of movies, they used rain when somebody was sad. What you constantly try to do is use the elements that you can to make a unifying

thread. The threads that run through a film that come together at the film's end are what generally stay in people's minds. They generally don't talk about the plot. They talk about what the elements and metaphors mean. Generally a film that moves you has a lot more going for it than what's on the surface.

Could you elaborate on how some of the special effects of The Exorcist *were accomplished?*

FRIEDKIN: I'm not going to give that away. A film works on an audience successfully because of its editing. If any of the people standing in line to see the film were to have stood in the studio watching the filming they would not have been impressed by the way in which we put the material together. I'll tell you two things: One, there are no optical effects, that is, achieved by any special printing process. They were all done live, including the vomit. The second thing I'll tell you is that the levitation was done without wires and involved the use of magnetic fields.

How did you decide on the quality of the voice for the demon?

FRIEDKIN: I have a cassette recording of an actual exorcism performed in Rome. It's in Italian. It involves the exorcism of a fourteen-year-old boy. I got the tape through the Jesuit Provincial of New York, and on the tape are the sounds produced by this young man supposedly possessed. The exorcism goes on for hours on this tape, and it's those sounds that I emulated for the demon. Because it was never clear to me in the novel nor was Blatty able to

Friedkin on location for *The Exorcist*

122

verbalize how the demon should sound, I made the decision to use a woman's voice for the demon and not a man. But I wanted a woman's voice that would be sharp, abrasive, and slightly neutral—by that I mean neither male nor female. Certainly not a voice that anyone could say: "Oh, that's just a man's voice." To give you an idea of what a voice sounds like while under the influence of a so-called demonic possession—it generally gets deeper, gravely. If you've ever seen anyone having an epileptic fit, the voice takes on that character. Demonic possession is close to epilepsy, emphysema, the cursing disease, but it is when many supernatural events surround the victim that they know it's none of the above.

Are you completely satisfied with the way The Exorcist *turned out?*

FRIEDKIN: I would always change everything I've done if I had the opportunity. But then I never do. Once I've finished a picture and delivered it to the studio, I make it a very special point that "that's it." Especially if it seems to be working. It's like Barbra Streisand. She's out in the street working with a broken nose. Everybody told her before she started, "Go fix your nose, it'll never work." And she's out there in the street working and she's a hit. So why fix it? There are a lot of technical faults in *The Exorcist* and *The French Connection* that I'm aware of, that for laziness or whatever else, I wasn't able to correct. I now am able to correct them; they'd let me. But I won't do it if it's working for the audience. I just take this attitude and say: "I've made this picture, that's the best I could do at this stage of my ability, and to hell with it." I'll try and fix what I know is wrong with the film on the next film I make.

Can you tell me what fear is and how you try to deal with it in your films?

FRIEDKIN: Yes, I can talk about it anyway. There's a difference between rational and irrational fear. I've tried to explore both in a couple of pictures. *The Birthday Party* happens to be about irrational fear. Irrational fear is a bit more difficult to deal with because it involves paranoia. To simplify it, *The Birthday Party* is about five people in a room, and somebody says something and one person in the room thinks it is funny, the other pays no attention to it at all, somebody else is shocked by what is said, and the other person is terrified for no apparent reason because what was said has struck some chord in this person that goes so deep he can't even communicate the reason for his fear even to himself.

Makeup artist Dick Smith coming to terms with the problem of turning a teenage girl into a demonically possessed monster

Irrational fear, which we all go through, is deep seated and psychological. It would take years of analysis to get to. Why, for example, when you go to a party and there are 150 people enjoying themselves, do you feel absolutely terrified of social contact? Rational fear, on the other hand, is induced by something called expectancy set, which is the personal feeling that something terrifying is going to happen to you. For example, you're walking down the street at night and you're convinced, not for reasons of paranoia, that someone is following you. So every sound you hear, whether it's a car coming around the corner, or leaves on the street, or a twig breaking under your foot, or footsteps, everything contributes to your fear, and this is because you're expecting to be frightened. The cinema takes advantage of this factor. Alfred Hitchcock takes advantage of the fact that an audience comes into the theatre expecting to be scared. When they are standing in line they are afraid. So he takes them for about an hour and dangles them and lets them do it for themselves until he hits them with something— and at that point, when he hits them, he either fulfills their expectations and fantasy or he lets them down, depending on how skillful is his punch. The same is true for *The Exorcist*. People are afraid while they're standing in line. And for the first hour of the film, while there is little more than exposition and some of that very hard to follow unless you've read the book, people are working themselves into an emotional state that is inducive to becoming ter-

123

rified. Those are the factors that contribute to fear. Fear is generally something that is behind you, speaking in psychological terms. It's generally something behind you that you cannot see but that you can feel, like a loud sound or someone touching you suddenly. Or it's something behind the door that's about to be opened. Most of the nightmares that you read about someone having involve someone coming up to a closed door behind which there is the unknown. Another factor, in more physical terms, would be a cold chill on the back of the neck, be it a hand or a chill when there is no cold. That's what fear is and does. Not so much the butterflies in your stomach, which come from anxiety, but that feeling on the back of your neck: a chill.

What particular directors do you admire?

FRIEDKIN: Of working directors, I particularly admire Kubrick, and of directors who are no longer active, Raoul Walsh. There are a lot of films I like, but I wouldn't necessarily say that everything that those directors have made I admire. For instance, *Citizen Kane* is the best film I've ever seen, but I don't like most of Welles' other work. I don't even relate the intelligence of *Citizen Kane* to the intelligence of *The Magnificent Ambersons*. I like *Treasure of Sierra Madre*, but not too much else of John Huston's. *All About Eve, Paths of Glory, 8½, White Heat, 2001, L'Aventura*, these are the movies I use a lot, by that I mean, look at and assimilate.

Do you consider yourself an auteur?

FRIEDKIN: No, just a filmmaker.

APPENDIX 2
FILMOGRAPHIES

THE HORROR-OF-PERSONALITY
FILMOGRAPHY

This list includes the horror-of-personality films (which are in capital letters) and those that either influenced or were influenced by the subgenre. In the credits, the D stands for director, S for screenwriter, P for producer, PH for photographer, M for music composer, AD for art director, SD for set designer. A name in parentheses indicates the author of the original source on which the screenplay was based, when important.

LES DIABOLIQUES (DIABOLIQUE)—1955, D:Henri-Georges Clouzot, S:Clouzot, Jerome Geronimi (Boileau and Narcejac), PH: Armand Thirard, AD:Leon Barsacq, M:Georges van Parys, with Paul Meurisse, Charles Vanel, Simone Signoret, Vera Clouzot.

SCREAMING MIMI—1958, D:Gerd Oswald, S:Robert Blees, PH:Burnett Guffey, SD:Frank A. Tuttle, with Anita Ekberg, Gypsy Rose Lee.

Screaming Skull—1958, D:Alex Nicol, S:John Kneubuhl, PH:Frank Crosley, M:Ernest Gould, with John Hudson, Peggy Webber.

I Bury the Living—1958, D:Albert Band, S:Louis Garfinkle, PH:Frederick Gately, M:Gerald Fried, with Richard Boone, Theodore Bikel.

Macabre—1958, D,P:William Castle, S:Robb White, PH:Carl E. Guthrie, M:Les Baxter, AD:Jack T. Collis and Robert Kinoshita, with William Prince, Jim Backus, Ellen Corby, Christine White.

Terror in the Haunted House—1958, D:Harold Daniels, S:Robert C. Dennis, PH:Frederick West, AD:A. Leslie Thomas, SD:Tom Oliphant, M:Darrell Calker, with Gerald Mohr, Cathy O'Donnell, William Ching, John Qualen.

House on Haunted Hill—1958, D,P:William Castle, S:Robb White, PH:Carl E. Guthrie, AD:David Milton, SD:Morris Hoffman, with Vincent Price, Carol Ohmart, Elisha Cook.

Horrors of the Black Museum—1959, D:Arthur Crabtree, P:Herman Cohen, S:Aben Kandel and Herman Cohen, PH: Desmond Dickinson, AD:Wilfred Arnold, M:Gerard Schurmann, with Michael Gough, June Cunningham.

The Bat—1959, D:Crane Wilbur, S:Crane Wilbur (Mary Roberts Rinehart), PH:Joseph Biroc, AD:David Milton, SD:Rudy Butler, M:Louis Forbes, with Vincent Price, Agnes Moorehead.

The Tingler—1959, D,P:William Castle, S:Robb White, PH:Wilfrid M. Cline, AD:Phil Bennett, SD:Milton Stumph, M:Von Dexter, with Vincent Price, Judith Evelyn.

The Hypnotic Eye—1960, D:George Blair, S:Gitta and William Read Woodfield, PH:Archie Dalzell, AD:David Milton, SD:Frank Wade, with Jacques Bergerac, Allison Hayes.

Circus of Horrors—1960, D:Sydney Hayers, S:George Baxt, PH:Douglas Slocombe, AD:Jack Shampan, with Anton Diffring, Erika Remberg.

PSYCHO—1960, D,P:Alfred Hitchcock, S:Joseph Stefano (Robert Bloch), PH:John J. Russell, AD:Joseph Hurley and Robert Clatworthy, SD:George Milo, M:Bernard Herrmann, with Anthony Perkins, Janet Leigh, Vera Miles, John Gavin, Martin Balsam, John McIntire, Frank Albertson, Patricia Hitchcock.

13 Ghosts—1960, D,P:William Castle, S:Robb White, PH:Joseph Biroc, M:Von Dexter, AD:Cary Odell, SD:Louise Diage, with Donald Woods, Charles Herbert, Jo Morrow.

Mania (originally called *The Flesh and the Fiends*)—1960, D:John Gilling, S:Gilling, Leon Griffiths, with Christopher Lee, Donald Pleasance.

Frantic (originally called *Ascenseur Pour L'Echafaud—Elevator to the Scaffold*)—1961 (released), D,S:Louis Malle, with Jeanne Moreau, Maurice Ronet.

HOMICIDAL—1961, D,P:William Castle, S:Robb White, PH:Burnett Guffey, AD:Cary Odell, SD:Darrell Silvera, M:Hugo Friedhoffer, with Glenn Corbett, Patricia Breslin, Eugenie Leontovich, Jean Arless.

SCREAM OF FEAR—1961, D:Seth Holt, S,P:Jimmy Sangster, PH:Douglas Slocombe, AD:Tom Goswell, M:Clifton Parker, with Susan Strasberg, Ronald Lewis, Ann Todd, Christopher Lee.

Mr. Sardonicus—1961, D,P:William Castle, S:Ray Russell, PH:Burnett Guffey, M:Von Dexter, AD:Cary Odell, SD:James M. Crowe, with Oscar Homolka, Guy Rolfe, Ronald Lewis, Audrey Dalton.

THE CABINET OF CALIGARI—1962, D,P:Robert Kay, S:Robert Bloch, PH:John Russell, M:Gerald Fried, SD:Howard Bristol, with Dan O'Herlihy, Glynis Johns, Constance Ford, Estelle Winwood.

WHAT EVER HAPPENED TO BABY JANE?—1962, D,P:Robert Aldrich, S:Lukas Heller (Henry Farrell), PH:Ernest Haller, M:Frank De Vol, AD:William Glasgow, SD:George Sawley, with Bette Davis, Joan Crawford, Victor Buono, Anna Lee.

PEEPING TOM—1962, D,P:Michael Powell, S:Leo Marks, PH:Otto Heller, with Carl Boehm, Moira Shearer, Anna Massey.

Trauma—1962, D,S:Robert Malcolm Young, P:Joseph Cranston, PH:Jacques Marquette, with John Conte, Lynn Bari, Lorrie Richards, Rudy Borner.

The Haunting—1963, D,P:Robert Wise, S:Nelson Gidding (Shirley Jackson), AD:Elliot Scott, SD:John Jarvis, with Julie Harris, Claire Bloom, Richard Johnson.

MANIAC—1963, D:Michael Carreras, S,P:Jimmy Sangster, PH:Wilkie Cooper, M:Stanley Black, AD:Edward Carrick, with Kerwin Mathews, Donald Houston, Nadia Gray, Liliane Brousse.

DEMENTIA 13—1963, D:Francis Ford Coppola, P:Roger Corman, PH:Charles Hannawalt, AD:Albert Locatelli, M:Ronald Stein, with William Campbell, Luana Anders, Patrick Magee, Bart Patton.

STRAIT-JACKET—1964, D,P:William Castle, S:Robert Bloch, PH:Arthur Arling, M:Van Alexander, AD:Boris Leven, SD:Frank Tuttle, with Joan Crawford, Diane Baker, Leif Erickson, Rochelle Hudson, George Kennedy.

Dead Ringer—1964, D:Paul Henreid, P:William H. Wright, S:Albert Beich and Oscar Millard, PH:Ernest Haller, M:André Previn, AD:Perry Ferguson, SD:William Stevens, with Bette Davis, Karl Malden, Peter Lawford.

Pyro—1964, D:Julio Coll, S:Sid Pink, with Barry Sullivan, Martha Hyer, Sherry Moreland, Hugo Pimentel.

Shock Treatment—1964, D:Denis Sanders, P:Aaron Rosenberg, S:Sydney Boehm, M:Jerry Goldsmith, PH:Sam Leavitt, AD:Jack Martin Smith and Hilyard Brown, SD:Walter M. Scott and Paul S. Fox, with Stuart Whitman, Lauren Bacall, Carol Lynley, Roddy McDowall.

NIGHTMARE—1964, D:Freddie Francis, S,P:Jimmy Sangster, PH:John Wilcox, M:Don Banks, AD:Bernard Robinson, with David Knight, Moira Redmond, Jennie Linden, Brenda Bruce.

LADY IN A CAGE—1964, D:Walter Grauman, S,P:Luther Davis, PH:Lee Garmes, AD:Rudolph Sternad, SD:Joseph Kish, with Olivia de Havilland, Ann Southern, James Caan, Jeff Corey, Jennifer Billingsley, Rafael Campos, Scat Man Cruthers, William Swan.

HUSH, HUSH, SWEET CHARLOTTE—1964, D,P:Robert Aldrich, S:Henry Farrell and Lukas Heller, PH:Joseph Biroc, M:Frank De Vol, AD:William Glasgow, Choreography: Alex Ruiz, Title Song:Mack David, with Bette Davis, Joseph Cotten, Olivia de Havilland, Agnes Moorehead, Mary Astor, Cecil Kellaway, William Campbell.

Marnie—1964, D,P:Alfred Hitchcock, S:Jay Presson Allen (Winston Graham), PH:Robert Burks, AD:Robert Boyle, George Milo, M:Bernard Herrmann, with Tippi Hedren, Sean Connery, Diane Baker, Martin Gabel, Louise Latham, Bruce Dern.

DIE, DIE, MY DARLING (FANATIC)—1965, D:Silvio Narizzano, S:Richard Matheson (Anne Blaisdell), P:Anthony Heads, with Tallulah Bankhead, Stefanie Powers, Yootha Joyce, Donald Sutherland.

WHO KILLED TEDDY BEAR?—1965, D:Joseph Cates, S:Leon Tokatyan, Arnold Drake, PH:Joseph Brun, with Sal Mineo, Juliet Prowse, Jan Murray, Elaine Stritch.

I Saw What You Did—1965, D,P:William Castle, S:William McGivern, with Joan Crawford, John Ireland, Leif Erickson, Sarah Lane, Patricia Breslin, John Crawford.

THE NANNY—1965, D:Seth Holt, S,P:Jimmy Sangster (Evelyn Piper), with Bette Davis, William Dix, Wendy Craig, Jill Bennett, James Villiers, Pamela Franklin.

REPULSION—1965, D:Roman Polanski, S:Polanski, Gerard Brach, P:Gene Gutowski, PH:Gilbert Taylor, with Catherine Deneuve, Yvonne Furneaux, John Fraser.

BUNNY LAKE IS MISSING—1965, D:Otto Preminger, S:John and Penelope Mortimer (Evelyn Piper), with Carol Lynley, Keir Dullea, Laurence Olivier, Noel Coward.

THE COLLECTOR—1965, D:William Wyler, P:Jud Kinberg and John Kohn, S:Stanley Mann and John Kohn (John Fowles), with Terence Stamp, Samantha Eggar.

THE PSYCHOPATH—1966, D:Freddie Francis, S:Robert Bloch, PH:John Wilcox, P:Max J. Rosenberg and Milton Subotsky, AD:Bill Constable, with

Olivia de Havilland in *Lady in a Cage*

Bette Davis and Wendy Craig in *The Nanny*

Patrick Wymark, Margaret Johnston, John Standing, Judy Huxtable, Don Borisenko, Alexander Knox.

PICTURE MOMMY DEAD—1966, D,P:Bert Gordon, S:Robert Sherman, PH:Ellsworth Fredericks, SD:Roy Moyer, with Don Ameche, Martha Hyer, Zsa Zsa Gabor, Susan Gordon, Maxwell Reed, Wendell Corey, Signe Hasso.

In Cold Blood—1967, D,S:Richard Brooks (Truman Capote), with Robert Blake, Scott Wilson, John Forsythe.

Psycho-Circus—1967, D:John Moxey, S:Peter Welbeck (Edgar Wallace), with Christopher Lee, Leo Genn, Anthony Newlands.

GAMES—1967, D:Curtis Harrington, S:Gene Kearney, P:George Edwards, PH:William A. Fraker, M:Samuel Matlovsky, AD:Alexander Golitzen and William D. De Cinces, SD:John McCarthy and James S. Redd, with Simone Signoret, James Caan, Katharine Ross, Don Stroud, Estelle Winwood, Kent Smith, Ian Wolfe, Florence Marly.

BERSERK—1968, D:Jim O'Connolly, S:Aben Kandel and Herman Cohen, P:Herman Cohen, PH:Desmond Dickinson, AD:Maurice Pelling, SD:Helen Thomas, M:John Scott, with Joan Crawford, Ty Hardin, Diana Dors, Judy Geeson.

TARGETS—1968, D,S:Peter Bogdanovich, PH:Laszlo Kovacs, PD:Polly Platt, with Boris Karloff, Tim O'Kelly, Sandy Baron, Peter Bogdanovich.

The Boston Strangler—1968, D:Richard Fleischer, S:Edward Anhalt, with Tony Curtis, George Kennedy, Henry Fonda, Mike Kellin.

PRETTY POISON—1968, D:Noel Black, S:Lorenzo Semple, Jr. (Stephen Geller), P:Lawrence Turman, Marshal Backlar, and Noel Black, M:Johnny Mandel, AD:Jack Martin Smith and Harold Michelson, with Anthony Perkins, Tuesday Weld, Beverly Garland, John Randolph, Dick O'Neill.

TWISTED NERVE—1968, D:Roy Boulting, S:Leo Marks and Roy Boulting, PH:Harry Waxman, M:Bernard Herrmann, AD:Albert Witherick, with Hayley Mills, Hywel Bennett, Billie Whitelaw, Phyllis Calvert.

THE MAD ROOM—1969, D:Bernard Girard, S:Girard and A.Z. Martin, P:Norman Maurer, M:David Grusin, AD:Sidney Litwack, SD:Sid Clifford, with Stella Stevens, Shelley Winters, Skip Ward, Carol Cole.

WHAT EVER HAPPENED TO AUNT ALICE?—1969, D:Lee H. Katzin, S:Theodore Apstein, PH:Joseph Biroc, M:Gerald Fried, P:Robert Aldrich and Peter Nelson, AD:William Glasgow, SD:John W. Brown, with Geraldine Page, Ruth Gordon, Rosemary Forsythe.

Paranoia (originally called Orgasmo)—1969, D:Umberto Lenzi, S:Lenzi, Ugo Moretti, Marie Sollenville, with Carroll Baker, Lou Castel, Tino Carraro.

Beverly Garland, Anthony Perkins, and Tuesday Weld in *Pretty Poison*

DADDY'S GONE A-HUNTING.—1969, D:Mark Robson, S:Larry Cohen, Lorenzo Semple, Jr., PH:Ernest Laszlo, M:John Williams, SD:Charles Thompson, with Carol White, Scott Hylands, Paul Burke, Mala Powers, Rachel Ames.

HOW AWFUL ABOUT ALLAN—1970, D:Curtis Harrington, S:Henry Farrell, PH:Fleet Southcott, P:George Edwards, M:Laurence Rosenthal, with Anthony Perkins, Joan Hackett, Julie Harris, Kent Smith.

PLAY MISTY FOR ME—1971, D:Clint Eastwood, S:Jo Heims, Dean Riesner, with Clint Eastwood, Jessica Walter, Donna Mills, John Larch, Don Siegel.

WHAT'S THE MATTER WITH HELEN?—1971, D:Curtis Harrington, S:Henry Farrell, PH:Lucien Ballard, P:George Edwards, M:David Raksin, AD:Eugene Lourie, with Shelley Winters, Debbie Reynolds, Dennis Weaver, Agnes Moorehead, Logan Ramsey.

10 Rillington Place—1971, D:Richard Fleischer, S:Clive Exton (Ludovic Kennedy), with Richard Attenborough, Judy Geeson, John Hart.

WHO SLEW AUNTIE ROO?—1972, D:Curtis Harrington, P:Louis M. Heyward, Samuel Z. Arkoff, and James H. Nicholson, S:Robert Blees and Jimmy Sangster, Gavin Lambert, PH:Desmond Dickinson, M:Kenneth V. Jones, AD:George Provis, with Shelley Winters, Mark Lester, Ralph Richardson, Lionel Jeffries, Hugh Griffith.

SEE NO EVIL—1972, D:Richard Fleischer, with Mia Farrow.

FRENZY—1972, D,P:Alfred Hitchcock, PH:Gil Taylor, S:Anthony Shaffer (Arthur La Bern), M:Ron Goodwin, Editor: John Jympson, with Jon Finch, Barry Foster, Anna Massey, Barbara Leigh-Hunt, Alec McGowan, Vivien Merchant, Bernard Cribbins, Billie Whitelaw.

IMAGES—1972, D:Robert Altman, P:Tommy Thompson, S:Altman, PH:Vilmos Zsigmond, AD:Leon Erickson, M:John Williams, Editor: Graeme Clifford, with Susannah York, René Auberjonois, Marcel Bozuffi, Hugh Millais, Cathryn Harrison.

SISTERS—1973, D:Brian de Palma, P:Edward R. Pressman, S:De Palma and Louisa Rose. PH:Gregory Sandow, M:Bernard Herrman, PD:Gary Weist, Editor:Paul Hirsch, with Margot Kidder, Jennifer Salt, Charles Durning, Bill Finley, Lisle Wilson, Barnard Hughes, Mary Davenport.

THE KILLING KIND—1974, D:Curtis Harrington, P:George Edwards, S:Tony Crechales and George Edwards, PH:Mario Losi, M:Andrew Belling, with Ann Southern, John Savage, Ruth Roman, Luana Anders, Cindy Williams.

THE LEGEND OF LIZZIE BORDEN—1974, D:Paul Wendkos, P:George LeMaire, S:William Bast, with Elizabeth Montgomery, Fionnuala Flanagan, Ed Flanders, Katherine Helmond, Don Porter, Fritz Weaver, Helen Craig, John Beal, Alan Hewitt, Bonnie Bartlett, Gail Kobe.

Shelley Winters in *Who Slew Auntie Roo?*

Margot Kidder in *Sisters*

REFLECTIONS OF MURDER—1974 (Remake of *Diabolique*) D: John Badham, with Joan Hackett, Tuesday Weld, Sam Waterston, Lucille Benson.

THE HORROR-OF-ARMAGEDDON FILMOGRAPHY

This list includes the horror-of-Armageddon films (which are in capital letters) and those that either influenced or were influenced by the subgenre. In the credits, the D stands for director, S for screenwriter, P for producer, PH for photographer, M for music composer, AD for art director, SD for set designer. A name in parentheses indicates the author of the original source on which the screenplay was based, when important.

The Thing—1951, D:Christian Nyby, P:Howard Hawks, with Margaret Sheridan, Kenneth Tobey, James Arness.

The Day the Earth Stood Still—1951, D:Robert Wise, with Michael Rennie, Patricia Neal.

Rod Taylor in *The Time Machine*

Joan Weldon in *Them*

Five—1951, D:Arch Oboler, with William Phipps, Susan Douglas.

THEM—1954, D:Gordon Douglas, with James Arness, James Whitmore, Edmund Gwenn.

Invasion of the Body Snatchers—1956, D:Don Siegel, P:Walter Wanger, S:Daniel Mainwaring, PH:Ellsworth Fredericks, with Kevin McCarthy, Dana Wynter.

BEGINNING OF THE END—1957, D:Bert I. Gordon, with Peter Graves, Peggie Castle, Morris Ankrum.

THE BLACK SCORPION—1957, D:Edward Ludwig, Special Effects: Willis O'Brien, with Richard Denning, Mara Corday, Carlos Rivas.

THE KILLER SHREWS—1959, D:Ray Kellogg, P:Ken Curtis, with James Best, Ingrid Goude.

On the Beach—1959, D,P:Stanely Kramer, with Gergory Peck, Ava Gardner, Fred Astaire, Anthony Perkins.

The World, the Flesh, and the Devil—1959, D:R. MacDougall, with Harry Belafonte, Inger Stevens, Mel Ferrer.

Hiroshima, Mon Amour—1960, D:Alain Resnais, with Emmanuele Riva, Eiji Okada, Stella Dassas, Pierre Barband.

The Time Machine—1960, D,P:George Pal, S:David Duncan (H.G.Wells), PH:Paul C. Vogel, AD:George W. Davis, with Rod Taylor, Yvette Mimieux.

Village of the Damned—1960, D:Wolf Rilla, P:Ronald Kinnoch, S:Stirling Silliphant, Wolf Rilla, George Barclays (John Wyndham's *The Midwich Cuckoos*), PH:Geoffrey Faithful, AD:Ivan Howard, with George Sanders.

"ANGER" in THE 7 CAPITAL SINS—1961, (one segment) D:Sylvain Dhomme, S:Eugène Ionesco.

The Damned—1961, D:Joseph Losey, with MacDonald Carey, Shirley Anne Field, Oliver Reed, Viveca Lindfors.

Panic in the Year Zero—1961, D:Ray Milland, with Ray Milland, Jean Hagen, Frankie Avalon.

THE BIRDS—1962, D,P:Alfred Hitchcock, S:Evan Hunter (Daphne du Maurier), PH:Robert Burks, Special Effects:Lawrence A. Hampton, Editor:George Tomasini, AD:Robert Boyle, George Milo, Sound Consultant:Bernard Herrmann, with Rod Taylor, Tippi Hedren, Jessica Tandy, Suzanne Pleshette.

DAY OF THE TRIFFIDS—1963, D:Steve Sekely, P:George Pitcher, S:Philip Yordan (John Wyndham), PH:Ted Moore, M:Ron Goodwin, AD:Cedric Dawe, with Howard Keel, Nicole Maurey.

LORD OF THE FLIES—1963, D,S:Peter Brook (William Golding), P:Lewis Allen, PH:Tom Hollyman, with James Aubrey, Tom Chapin, Hugh Edwards.

Ladybug, Ladybug—1963, D,P:Frank Perry, S:Eleanor Perry, PH:Leonard Hirschfield, AD:Albert Drenner, with Estelle Parsons, Judith Lowry, Alice Playten.

Dr. Strangelove—1964, D:Stanley Kubrick, with Peter Sellers, George C. Scott.

Fail-Safe—1964, D:Sidney Lumet, with Henry Fonda, Walter Matthau.

Last Man on Earth—1964, D:Sidney Salkow, with Vincent Price, Franca Bettoia.

Children of the Damned—1964, D:Anton M. Leader, S:John Briley, PH:David Boulton, AD:Elliot Scott, M:Ron Goodwin, with Ian Hendry, Barbara Ferris.

THE WAR GAME—1965, D,P,S:Peter Watkins, PH:Peter Bartlett.

The Bedford Incident—1965, D:James B. Harris, with Richard Widmark, Sidney Poitier, Martin Balsam, Wally Cox.

THE DEADLY BEES—1967, D:Freddie Francis, P:Max J. Rosenberg and Milton Subotsky, S:Robert Bloch and Anthony Marriott. PH:John Wilcos, AD:Bill Constable, with Suzanna Leigh, Frank Finlay.

Battle for the Planet of the Apes

PLANET OF THE APES—1968, D:Franklin J. Schaffner, S:Michael Wilson and Rod Serling (Pierre Boulle), PH:Leon Shamroy, AD:Jack Martin Smith, Makeup: John Chambers, with Charlton Heston, Roddy McDowall, Kim Hunter, Maurice Evans.

NIGHT OF THE LIVING DEAD—1968, D,PH:George A. Romero, P:Russell Streiner and Karl Hardman, S:John A. Russo, with Judith O'Dea, Russell Streiner, Duane Jones, Karl Hardman.

EYE OF THE CAT—1969, D:David Lowell Rich, P:Bernard Schwarts and Philip Hazelton, S:Joseph Stefano, PH:Russell Metty and Ellsworth Fredericks, M:Lalo Schifrin, AD:Alexander Golitzen and William De Cincies, with Michael Sarrazin, Gayle Hunnicut, Eleanor Parker.

THEY SHOOT HORSES, DON'T THEY?—1969, D:Sidney Pollack, with Jane Fonda, Gig Young, Red Buttons, Susannah York, Bonnie Bedelia.

BENEATH THE PLANET OF THE APES—1970, D:Ted Post, P:Arthur P. Jacobs, S:Paul Dehn, M:Leonard Rosenman, with James Franciscus, Kim Hunter, Maurice Evans, Linda Harrison.

Airport—1970, D:George Seaton, with Burt Lancaster, George Kennedy, Dean Martin, Helen Hayes.

WILLARD—1971, D:Daniel Mann, P:Mort Briskin, S:Gilbert A. Ralston (Stephen Gilbert), PH:Robert B. Hauser, M:Alex North, AD:Howard Hollander, Animals Trained by Moe and Nora DiSesso, with Bruce Davison, Elsa Lanchester, Ernest Borgnine, Sondra Locke.

ESCAPE FROM THE PLANET OF THE APES—1971, D:Don Taylor, P:Arthur P. Jacobs, S:Paul Dehn, PH:Joseph Biroc, with Roddy McDowell, Kim Hunter, Bradford Dillman.

The Omega Man—1971, D:Boris Segal, S:John William and Joyce Corrington (Richard Matheson), PH:Russell Metty, with Charlton Heston, Rosalind Cash.

THE PIED PIPER—1971, D:Jacques Demy, with Donovan.

THE HELLSTROM CHRONICLE—1971, D,P:Walon Green, Executive Producer:David Wolper, PH:Helmut Barth, Walon Green, Ken Middleham, Gerald Thompson, with Lawrence Pressman.

BEN—1972, D:Phil Karlson, P:Mort Briskin, S:Gilbert A. Ralston, PH:Russell Metty, AD:Rolland M. Brooks, with Lee Harcourt Montgomery.

CONQUEST OF THE PLANET OF THE APES—1972, D:J. Lee Thompson, P:Arthur P. Jacobs, S:Paul Dehn, PH:Bruce Surtees, M:Tom Scott, with Roddy McDowall, Don Murray, Natalie Trundy.

NIGHT OF THE LEPUS—1972, D:William F. Claxton, with Janet Leigh, Stuart Whitman.

FROGS—1972, D:George McCowan, P:George Edwards and Peter Thomas, Presented by Nicholson and Arkoff, S:Robert Hut Chisin and Robert Blees, PH:Mario Tosi, with Ray Milland, Sam Elliot.

The Poseidon Adventure—1972, D:Ronald Neame, P:Irwin Allen, with Gene Hackman, Shelley Winters, Ernest Borgnine.

BATTLE FOR THE PLANET OF THE APES—1973, D:J. Lee Thompson, P:Arthur P. Jacobs, S:John William and Joyce Corrington, PH:Richard H. Kline, M:Leonard Rosenman, with Roddy McDowall, Claude Akins, Natalie Trundy.

RHINOCEROS—1973, D:Tom O'Horgan, P:Ely Landau, American Film Theatre, S:Julian Berry (Eugène Ionesco), with Gene Wilder, Karen Black, Zero Mostel, Joe Silver, Percy Rodrigues, Robert Weil, Marilyn Chris.

THE KILLER BEES—1974, D:Curtis Harrington, with Gloria Swanson.

Juggernaut—1974, D:Richard Lester, with Richard Harris, Omar Sharif.

Genevieve Bujold in *Earthquake*

PHASE IV—1974, D:Saul Bass, P:Paul B. Radin, S:Mayo Simon, PH:Dick Bush, with Nigel Davenport.

Airport 75—1974, with Charlton Heston, George Kennedy, Karen Black, Gloria Swanson, Helen Reddy, Linda Blair.

Earthquake—1974, D,P:Mark Robson, S:George Fox and Mario Puzo, PH:Philip Lathrop, PD:Alexander Golitzen, AD:E. Preston, M:John Williams, Special Photography: Clifford Stine, Matte Photography:Ross Hoffman, Miniatures: G. Robinson, Stunts: John Daheim, Special Effects: Frank Brendel, Sound:Melvin M. Metcalfe Sr., Ronald Pierce, with Charlton Heston, Ava Gardner, George Kennedy, Lorne Greene, Genevieve Bujold, Richard Roundtree, Marjoe Gortner, Barry Sullivan, Lloyd Nolan, Victoria Principal, Walter Matuschanskayasky (Walter Matthau).

The Towering Inferno—1974, D:John Guillerman and Irwin Allen, P:Irwin Allen, S:Stirling Silliphant, with Paul Newman, Steve McQueen, Faye Dunaway, Richard Chamberlain, William Holden, Susan Blakely, Jennifer Jones, Fred Astaire, Robert Wagner.

JAWS—1975, D:Steven Spielberg, P:Richard D. Zanuck and David Brown, S:Peter Benchley and Carl Gottlieb (Peter Benchley), M:John Williams, PH:Bill Butler, Editor: Verna Fields, Special Effects: Robert Matty, with Robert Shaw, Roy Scheider, Richard Dreyfuss, Lorraine Gary, Murray Hamilton, Peter Benchley.

BUG—1975, D:Jeannot Szwarc, P:Willian Castle, S:William Castle and Thomas Page (The Hephaestus Plague by Page), M:Charles Fox, with Bradford Dillman, Joanna Miles, Jamie Smith Jackson.

TIDAL WAVE—1975, (an American alteration of the Japanese The Destruction of Tokyo) American version with Lorne Greene.

The Hindenburg—1975, D,P:Robert Wise, S:Nelson Gidding, PH:Robert Surtees, AD:Ed Carfagno, SD:Frank McKelvy, with George C. Scott, Anne Bancroft, William Atherton, Gig Young, Roy Thinnes, Burgess Meredith.

THE SWARM—1977, P:Irwin Allen, S:Stirling Silliphant.

The Japanese Variety
(Toho Studios)

GODZILLA, KING OF THE MONSTERS—1956, D:Inoshiro Honda, with Raymond Burr, Takashi Shimura, Akira Takarada, Akihiko Hirato.

RODAN—1957, D:Inoshiro Honda, with Kenji Sawara, Akihiko Hirato.

THE MYSTERIANS—1959, D:Inoshiro Honda, with Kenji Sawara, Akihiko Hirato.

MOTHRA—1961, D:Inoshiro Honda, P:Tomoyuki Tanaka, S:Shinichi Sekizawa, Special Effects:Eiji Tsuburaya, with the Itoh Sisters.

Rodan

KING KONG VS. GODZILLA—1962, D:Inoshiro Honda, with Michael Keith and Tadeo Takashima.

MONSTER ZERO—1962, D:Inoshiro Honda.

WARNING FROM SPACE—1963, with Bontaro Miake, Shozu Nanbu, Mieko Nagai, Isao Yamagata, Toyomi Karita.

GODZILLA VS. THE THING—1964, D:Inoshiro Honda, with Akira Takarada.

GHIDRAH, THE 3-HEADED MONSTER—1965, D:Inoshiro Honda, with Yosuke Natsuki, Hiroshi Koizumi.

FRANKENSTEIN CONQUERS THE WORLD—1966, D:Inoshiro Honda, with Nick Adams, Tadeo Takashima, Kumi Mizuno.

GODZILLA'S REVENGE—1967, D:Inoshiro Honda.

KING KONG ESCAPES—1967, D:Inoshiro Honda, P:Tomoyuki Tanaka, S:Kaoru Mabuchi, with Rhodes Reason.

DESTROY ALL MONSTERS—1967, D:Inoshiro Honda, P:Tomoyuki Tanaka, S:Kaoru Mabucki, Ishiro Honda, PH:Taiichi Kankura, AD:Takeo Kita, Special Effects:Eiji Tsuburaya and Sadamasa Arikawa, with Akira Kubo.

YOG—MONSTER FROM SPACE—1970, D:Ishiro Honda, P:Tomoyuki Tanaka and Fumio Tanaka, PH:Taiichi Kankura, AD: Takeo Kita, with Akira Kubo.

GODZILLA VS. HEDORAH, THE SMOG MONSTER—1970, D:Yoshimitu Banno, P:Tomoyuki Tanaka, S:Kaoru Mabuchi and Yoshimitu Banno, PH:Yoishi Manoda, AD:Taiko Inoue, Special Effects: Shokei Nakano.

THE DESTRUCTION OF TOKYO—1974.

THE HORROR-OF-THE-DEMONIC FILMOGRAPHY

This list includes the horror-of-the-demonic films (which are in capital letters) and those that either influenced or were influenced by the subgenre. In the credits, the D stands for director, S for screenwriter, P for producer, PH for photographer, M for music composer, AD for art director, SD for set designer. A name in parentheses indicates the author of the original source on which the screenplay was based, when important.

DAY OF WRATH—1943, D:Carl Dreyer, PH:Karl Andersson, M:Paul Schierbeck, with Lisabeth Movin, Thorkild Roose.

133

The Itoh Sisters in *Ghidrah, the 3-Headed Monster*

The Devil's Wanton—1948, D:Ingmar Bergman, PH:Goran Strindberg, with Doris Svedlund, Birger Malmsten.

The Bad Seed—1956, D:Mervyn LeRoy, with Nancy Kelly, Patty McCormack.

HORROR HOTEL—1960, D:John Moxley, P:Donald Taylor, S:George Baxt, AD:John Blezard, with Patricia Jessel, Betta St. John, Christopher Lee.

THE INNOCENTS—1961, D:Jack Clayton, S:William Archibald and Truman Capote (Henry James), PH:Freddie Francis, AD:Wilfred Shingleton, with Deborah Kerr, Pamela Franklin, Martin Stephens.

BURN, WITCH, BURN—1962, D:Sidney Hayers, S:Charles Beaumont, Richard Matheson, George Baxt, AD:Jack Shampan, with Janet Blair, Peter Wyngarde.

"MORELLA" in TALES OF TERROR—1962, D:Roger Corman, S:Richard Matheson (Poe), PH:Floyd Crosby, AD:Daniel Haller, with Vincent Price.

DIARY OF A MADMAN—1963, D:Reginald LeBorg, P:Robert E. Kent, S:Kent (de Maupassant), PH:Ellis W. Carter, AD:Daniel Haller, with Vincent Price, Nancy Kovack.

THE HAUNTING—1963, D,P:Robert Wise, S:Nelson Gidding (Shirley Jackson), AD:Elliot Scott, SD:John Jarris, with Julie Harris, Claire Bloom, Richard Johnson.

THE HAUNTED PALACE—1964, D,P:Roger Corman, S:Charles Beaumont, PH:Floyd Crosby, AD:Daniel Haller, with Vincent Price, Debra Paget.

WITCHCRAFT—1964, D:Don Sharp, P:Robert Lippert and Jack Parsons, S:Harry Spaulding, PH:Arthur Lavis, AD:George Provis, with Lon Chaney, Jr.

THE DEVIL'S OWN—1966, D:Cyril Frankel, P:Anthony Nelson-Keys, PH:Arthur Grant, S:Nigel Kneale, AD:Don Mingaye, with Joan Fontaine, Alec McCowen, Gwen Ffrangcon-Davies.

EYE OF THE DEVIL—1967, D:J. Lee Thompson, P:John Calley, Martin Ransohoff, S:Robin Estridge, Dennis Murphy, PH:Erwin Hillier, AD:Elliot Scott, with Deborah Kerr, David Niven.

ROSEMARY'S BABY—1968, D:Roman Polanski, P:William Castle, S:Polanski (Ira Levin), M:Christopher Komeda, Production Design: Richard Sylbert, AD:Joel Schiller, with Mia Farrow, John Cassavetes, Ruth Gordon.

134

Yog—Monster from Outer Space

Deborah Kerr in *Eye of the Devil*

"NEVER BET THE DEVIL YOUR HEAD or TONY DAMMIT" in *SPIRITS OF THE DEAD*—1968, (segment) D:Federico Fellini, S:Fellini and Bernardino Zapponi, PH:Giuseppe Rotunno, M:Nino Rota, AD:Piero Tosi, with Terence Stamp and Marian Yaru.

THE DEVIL'S BRIDE—1968, D:Terence Fisher, P:Anthony Nelson Keys, S:Richard Matheson, PH:Arthur Grant, AD:Bernard Robinson, with Christopher Lee, Gwen Ffrangcon-Davies.

THE WITCHFINDER GENERAL—1968, D:Michael Reeves, with Vincent Price.

CROWHAVEN FARM—1970, D,P:Walter Grauman, S:John McGreevey, PH:Fleet Southcoat, AD:Tracy Bousman, with Hope Lange, Paul Burke, William Smith.

NIGHT OF DARK SHADOWS—1971, D,P:Dan Curtis, PH:Richard Shore, S:Sam Hall, AD:Trevor Williams, with David Selby, Kate Jackson.

THE BLOOD ON SATAN'S CLAW—1971, D:Piers Haggard, P:Peter L. Andrews and Malcolm B. Heyworth, S:Robert Wynne-Simons, AD:Arnold Chapkis.

EQUINOX—1971, D,S:Jack Woods, P:Jack H. Harris, PH:Mike Hoover.

THE BROTHERHOOD OF SATAN—1971, D:Bernard McEveety, P:L.Q. Jones and Alvy Moore, S:William Welch, PH:John Arthur Morrill, Production Design: Ray Boyle, with Strother Martin, L. Q. Jones.

MACBETH—1971, D:Roman Polanski, P:Andrew Braunsberg, S:Polanski, Kenneth Tynan (Shakespeare), PH:Gilbert Taylor, AD:Fred Carter, with Jon Finch, Francesca Annis.

THE MEPHISTO WALTZ—1971, D:Paul Wendkos, P:Quinn Martin, S:Ben Maddow (Fred Mustard Stewart), PH:William W. Spencer, M:Jerry Goldsmith, AD:Richard Y. Haman, with Alan Alda, Jacqueline Bisset, Barbara Parkins, Curt Jurgens.

SIMON, KING OF THE WITCHES—1971, D:Bruce Kessler, P:David Hammond, S:Robert Phippeny, PH:David Butler, AD:Dale Hennesy, with Andrew Prine, Brenda Scott.

MARK OF THE DEVIL—1972, D:Michael Armstrong, P:Adrian Hoven, S:Percy Parker, PH:Ernst W. Kalinke.

THE NIGHTCOMERS—1972, D,P:Michael Winner, S:Michael Hastings, PH:Robert Paynter, AD:Herbert Westbrook, with Marlon Brando.

THE POSSESSION OF JOEL DELANEY—1972, D:Waris Hussein, S:Matt Robinson and Grimes Grice, AD:Philip Rosenberg, with Shirley MacLaine, Perry King.

THE OTHER—1972, D,P:Robert Mulligan, S:Thomas Tryon (Tryon), PH:Robert L. Surtees, M:Jerry Goldsmith, Production Design: Albert Brenner, with Chris Udvarnoky, Martin Udvarnoky, Uta Hagen.

Chris Udvarnoky and Uta Hagen in *The Other*

Perry King in *The Possession of Joel Delaney*

CHILD'S PLAY—1972, D:Sidney Lumet, P:David Merrick, S:Leon Prochnik (Robert Marasco), PH:Gerald Hirschfeld, with James Mason, Robert Preston, Beau Bridges.

THE DEVIL'S DAUGHTER—1973, with Shelley Winters.

THE PYX—1973, D:Harvey Hart, P:Maxine Samuels and Julian Roffman, S:Robert Schlitt, with Karen Black, Christopher Plummer, Donald Pilon, Lee Broker.

DON'T LOOK NOW—1973, D:Nicolas Roeg, P:Peter Katz, S:Alan Scott and Chris Bryant (Daphne du Maurier), PH:Anthony Richmond, AD:Giovanni Soccol, SD: Francesco Chinanese, M:Pino Donnagio, with Julie Christie, Donald Sutherland, Hilary Mason, Massimo Serato, Renato Scarpa, Adelina Poerio.

THE EXORCIST—1973, D:William Friedkin, S:William Peter Blatty (Blatty), Makeup:Dick Smith, with Linda Blair, Mercedes McCambridge (as the voice of the devil), Ellen Burstyn, Max Von Sydow, Jason Miller.

THE STRANGER WITHIN—1974, D:Lee Philips, P:Neil T. Maffeo, S:Richard Matheson, with Barbara Eden, George Grizzard, Joyce Van Patten, David Doyle, Nehemiah Persoff.

ABBY—1974, with William Marshall, Carol Speed.

Donald Sutherland and Julie Christie in *Don't Look Now*

Sharon Farrell in *It's Alive!*

IT'S ALIVE!—1974, D, P,S: Larry Cohen, PH:Fenton Hamilton, Editor: Peter Honess, M:Bernard Herrmann, with John Ryan, Sharon Farrell, Andrew Duggan, Guy Stockwell, James Dixon, Michael Ansara.

TRILOGY OF TERROR—1975, P,D:Dan Curtis, "Amelia" segment written by Richard Matheson, other segments written by William F. Nolan from a story by Richard Matheson, with Karen Black, Robert Burton, John Karlin.

THE REINCARNATION OF PETER PROUD—1975, with Michael Sarrazin, Margot Kidder.

RACE WITH THE DEVIL—1975, D:Jack Starrett, P:Wes Bishop, S:Lee Frost and Wes Bishop, M:Leonard Rosenman, with Peter Fonda, Warren Oates, Loretta Swit, Lara Parker.

THE DEVIL'S RAIN—1975, D:Robert Fuest, P:James V. Cullen and Michael S. Glick, S:Gabe Essoe, James Ashton, Gerald Hopman, with Ernest Borgnine, Eddie Albert, William Shatner, Keenan Wynn, Tom Skerritt, Joan Prather, Ida Lupino.

BEYOND THE DOOR—1975, D:Oliver Hellman, S:Richard Barrett, M:Ortolani, with Juliet Mills, Richard Johnson, Elizabeth Turner, David Colin Jr., Gabriele Lavia.

THEY CAME FROM WITHIN—1976, P:Ivan Reitman, S,D:David Greenberg, with Paul Hampton, Joe Silver, Lynn Lowry, Barbara Steele.

NIGHT CHILD—1976, D,S:Max Dallamano, with Richard Johnson, Joanna Cassidy, Lila Kedrova, Edmund Purdom, Nicole Elmi.

TO THE DEVIL A DAUGHTER—1976, D:Peter Sykes, P:Roy Skeggs, S:Chris Wicking, PH:David Watkin, AD:Don Picton, with Richard Widmark, Christopher Lee, Honor Blackman, Denholm Elliott.

THE PREMONITION—1976, P,D:Robert Allen Schnitzer, S:Anthony Mahon and Schnitzer, with Sharon Farrell, Richard Lynch, Jeff Corey.

THE DEVIL WITHIN HER—1976, D:Peter Sasdy, S:Stanley Price, PH:Kenneth Talbot, AD:Roy Stannard, with Joan Collins, Eileen Atkins, Donald Pleasance, Ralph Bates, Caroline Munro.

BURNT OFFERINGS—1976, (Robert Marasco) with Karen Black, Oliver Reed, Bette Davis.

THE OMEN—1976, D:Richard Donner, P:Harvey Bernhard, S:David Seltzer, M:Jerry Goldsmith, with Gregory Peck, Lee Remick, David Warner, Billie Whitelaw.

BIBLIOGRAPHY

The following bibliography should prove useful to the reader interested in the cinema in general and the horror film in particular.

Abastado, Claude, *Eugene Ionesco*, Paris, Bordas, 1971.

Blatty, William Peter, *The Exorcist*, New York, Bantam Books, 1971.

Bloch, Robert, *Psycho*, New York, Bantam Books, 1959.

Butler, Ivan, *Horror in the Cinema*, New York, A. S. Barnes and Co., 1967.

Clarens, Carlos, *Horror Movies*, London, Secker and Warburg, 1968.

Cowie, Peter, ed., *A Concise History of the Cinema*, New York, A. S. Barnes and Co., 1971.

Esslin, Martin, *Theatre of the Absurd*, Garden City, Anchor Books, 1961.

Film Facts, ed. by Ernest Parmentier, Vol. I–XV, 1958–1972.

Frye, Northrop, *Anatomy of Criticism: Four Essays*, Princeton, Princeton University Press, 1957.

Halliwell, Leslie, *The Filmgoer's Companion*, New York, Equinox, 1970.

Higham, Charles, and Greenberg, Joel, *The Celluloid Muse: Hollywood Directors Speak*, New York, New American Library, 1969.

Huss, Roy Gerard, ed., and Ross, T.J., ed., *Focus on the Horror Film*, Englewood Cliffs, New Jersey, Prentice-Hall, 1972.

Ionesco, Eugène, *Jeux de Massacre*, Paris, Gallimard, 1970.

Ionesco, Eugène, "The Playwright's Role," *Observer*, 1970.

Ionesco, Eugène, *Plays*, Vol. I–VII, translated by Donald Watson, London, John Calder.

Kaminsky, Stuart M., *Don Siegel: Director*, New York, Curtis Books, 1974.

Knight, Arthur, *The Liveliest Art*, New York, New American Library, 1957.

Kracauer, Siegfried, *From Caligari to Hitler*, Princeton, Princeton University Press, 1947.

LaValley, Albert J., ed., *Focus on Hitchcock*, Englewood Cliffs, New Jersey, Prentice-Hall, 1972.

MacCann, Richard Dyer, ed., *Film: A Montage of Theories*, New York, E. P. Dutton and Co., 1966.

Maltin, Leonard, ed., *TV Movies*, New York, New American Library, 1969.

Michael, Paul, *American Movies Reference Book: The Sound Era*, London, Prentice-Hall, 1969.

Perkins, V.F., *Film as Film*, Middlesex, England, Penguin Books, 1972.

Quigley, Martin Jr., and Gertner, Richard, *Films in America*, New York, Golden Press, 1970.

Sarris, Andrew, *The American Cinema*, New York, E.P. Dutton and Co., 1968.

Styan, J.L., *The Dark Comedy*, Cambridge, Cambridge University Press, 1962.

Taylor, John Russell, *Cinema Eye, Cinema Ear*, New York, Hill and Wang, 1964.

Wood, Robin, *Hitchcock's Films*, New York, A. S. Barnes and Co., 1965.

Index